From Quality to Business Excellence

A Systems Approach to Management

Also Available from ASQ Quality Press:

The Executive Guide to Improvement and Change
G. Dennis Beecroft, Grace L. Duffy, and John W. Moran

The Change Agent's Guide to Radical Improvement
Ken Miller

*The Change Agents' Handbook: A Survival Guide for
Quality Improvement Champions*
David W. Hutton

Managing Change: Practical Strategies for Competitive Advantage
Kari Tuominen

Quality Problem Solving
Gerald F. Smith

Root Cause Analysis: Simplified Tools and Techniques
Bjørn Andersen and Tom Fagerhaug

Principles and Practices of Organizational Performance Excellence
Thomas J. Cartin

Six Sigma Project Management: A Pocket Guide
Jeffrey Lowenthal

*Customer Centered Six Sigma: Linking Customers,
Process improvement, and Financial Results*
Earl Naumann and Steven H. Hoisington

ISO 9001:2000 for Small and Medium Sized Businesses
Herbert C. Monnich, Jr.

The Certified Quality Manager Handbook, Second Edition
Duke Okes and Russell T. Westcott, editors

To request a complimentary catalog of ASQ Quality Press publications,
call 800-248-1946, or visit our Web site at http://qualitypress.asq.org .

From Quality to Business Excellence

A Systems Approach to Management

Charles G. Cobb

ASQ Quality Press
Milwaukee, Wisconsin

From Quality to Business Excellence
Charles G. Cobb

Library of Congress Cataloging-in-Publication Data

Cobb, Charles G., 1945–
   From quality to business excellence : a systems approach to management
/ Charles G. Cobb.
      p.   cm.
   Includes bibliographical references (p.   ) and index.
   ISBN 0-87389-578-9
   1. Total quality management.   2. Organizational effectiveness.   I. Title.

   HD62.15.C563   2003
   658.4'013—dc21

                                                    2002156211

10 9 8 7 6 5 4 3

ISBN 0-87389-578-9

Publisher: William Tony
Acquisitions Editor: Annemieke Koudstaal
Project Editor: Paul O'Mara
Production Administrator: Gretchen Trautman
Special Marketing Representative: David Luth

ASQ Mission: The American Society for Quality advances individual and organizational performance excellence worldwide by providing opportunities for learning, quality improvement, and knowledge exchange.

Attention: Bookstores, Wholesalers, Schools and Corporations: ASQ Quality Press books, videotapes, audiotapes, and software are available at quantity discounts with bulk purchases for business, educational, or instructional use. For information, please contact ASQ Quality Press at 800-248-1946, or write to ASQ Quality Press, P.O. Box 3005, Milwaukee, WI 53201-3005.

To place orders or to request a free copy of the ASQ Quality Press Publications Catalog, including ASQ membership information, call 800-248-1946. Visit our web site at www.asq.org or http://qualitypress.asq.org .

Printed in the United States of America

 Printed on acid-free paper

American Society for Quality

Quality Press
600 N. Plankinton Avenue
Milwaukee, Wisconsin 53203
Call toll free 800-248-1946
Fax 414-272-1734
www.asq.org
http://qualitypress.asq.org
http://standardsgroup.asq.org
E-mail: authors@asq.org

Dedication and Acknowledgements

I would like to dedicate this book to the memory of Professor Charley Osborn. Charley was my faculty adviser at Babson College when I did much of the studies and research that ultimately led to this book. Charley was a man of unbounded energy, enthusiasm, and vision. He received numerous faculty awards at Babson for the inspiring leadership he provided to many students. He fought bravely against Lou Gehrig's disease (ALS) and passed away late in 2001. He will be sadly missed by the many people he inspired, including me.

I want to acknowledge the faculty and staff of Babson College, where I received a Certificate in Advanced Management in 1998. Babson is noted among business schools for entrepreneurship and encourages students to develop and explore new ideas. A number of people on the Babson faculty encouraged me and helped me to develop many of the ideas in this book. Dave Kopcso was one of my professors at Babson and jointly wrote a paper with me on the Microsoft ".Net" architecture that was used as the basis of the section in this book on "Standards-Based Business Processes and Systems." Dave's courses always "pushed" the envelope of new technology and helped students see how to apply it to business situations. Bob Reck was also a big inspiration early in my studies at Babson in the reengineering area, and Donna Stoddard sponsored the work I did as a research associate on ERP systems that is the basis of some of the material in chapter 7.

There are many people who contributed to the development of the ideas in this book that I would like to specifically recognize:

- Jerry Butler—Jerry has been my manager at several points in my career and has given me a lot of good advice and mentoring over the years. In particular, he was the Vice President of Operations at Brite Voice Systems when I was working for him as the Director of

Quality, and he knows first hand how difficult this is to put into actual practice. Jerry's advice and input in the development of this book has been invaluable.

- Lav Gandhi, Bill Bishop, and Dorothy Crooks are colleagues of mine who fully understand these concepts and are working to put them into practice through the Ellicott Group and the Business Excellence Group. They reviewed the manuscript for this book and made a number of contributions to its content. Bill led a very large business system project with Daimler-Chrysler Services Asia Pacific that is documented in Chapter 4.

Numerous other people reviewed the manuscript for this book and provided helpful comments, suggestions, and inputs, including:

- Mike Katzorke and Bryan Blunt at Cessna Aircraft

- Marty Lustig and Robin Carlson at Sprint

- Leanne McAlister at Daimler-Chrysler Services Asia Pacific

- Gene Hutchison at SBC

- Roger Quayle at OMI

- Marty Snyder at Avaya

- Jack Aiken; Steve Curran; and my wife, Donna Caswell-Cobb

I also want to acknowledge the many customers I have worked with over the past four years who have given me the opportunity to work with them and to put some of these ideas into practice. And, finally, I want to acknowledge the many quality professionals and management consultants who have developed the foundation of knowledge that exists today. This book builds on the ideas of many others and synthesizes those ideas into an overall vision. Without their work and contribution, this book would not have been possible.

Table of Contents

Preface

I entered the quality profession late in my career, after 18 years with Digital Equipment Corporation where I held a variety of operational management, professional services, and engineering roles related to information systems. My interest in quality has always been in integrating quality with business and operational management. I spent several years with Motorola managing a group of people who were responsible for customer satisfaction and business process improvement and I then became Director of Corporate Quality for Brite Voice Systems.

After achieving ISO 9000 certification at Brite Voice Systems in 1997, I began to wonder where the future career direction for a Quality Manager was—and it wasn't very clear. The questions I set out to try and answer at that time have taken on an even broader significance today.

- We have gone through a dizzying array of management fads, quality standards, IT technologies, and so on. What comes next?

- People are still very confused about how all this fits together, and where it is going.

- American business is in a state of crisis:

  - Accounting scandals and lack of public confidence

  - Struggling to survive a very difficult recession

- How do we get out of this mess?

- What is the future going to look like?

I have spent a lot of time over the past 5–6 years doing a very extensive research project that ultimately led to this book, and then working with companies as a consultant to try to understand their future direction and to put some of these ideas into practice.

This book presents a "vision" for the future direction of quality management:

- *Quality* is taking on a broader meaning. It is no longer limited to a narrow perspective associated with reduction of defects in manufacturing. It includes all aspects of making a business more effective and improving customer satisfaction and loyalty, such as cycle time reduction, cost savings, and so on. Many of these areas may have been perceived as outside the realm of "quality" in the past.

- Many companies who are implementing this broader definition of quality call it *business excellence* because the word *quality* has a narrower connotation that has been associated with the quality of products and services a company produces and has become well engrained in people's thinking.

The implications of implementing this vision of the future are broad and far-reaching; it requires rethinking the way business management systems, quality management systems, and information systems are defined and implemented, and it requires a systems engineering approach to create a common understanding of how the overall business management system works and is improved continuously.

A very strong cross-functional management approach is needed. No single discipline within an organization has the breadth of knowledge or influence to unilaterally define and implement the integrated, cross-functional approach that's needed to solve these problems.

- "Quality" is no longer something that can be delegated to the quality control department to manage. It must be an integral part of the way the business is managed and requires very strong, cross-functional leadership at the highest levels in the company.

- By the same token, *information technology* is no longer something that can be delegated to the IT Department. It's becoming increasingly difficult, if not impossible, to separate the definition of the business processes from the systems that are associated with implementing them.

WHAT YOU'LL GET FROM THIS BOOK

This book does not pretend to offer a "canned" solution. There is no simple, "cookbook" solution, and the exact nature of any solution will vary significantly by industry, by company, and with many other factors. A business is a complex system and there are many complex systems that will never be fully understood (the human body is a good example). However, an understanding of how some of the major elements of the system work and interrelate is an essential starting point.

This book will show you how to integrate a management approach, any relevant quality standards, continuous improvement methodologies, and information technology into a management system designed to achieve business excellence. It also includes an approach to evaluate the maturity of your business management approach, to identify gaps that inhibit the effectiveness of your organization, and to develop an action plan for moving your organization to the next level of effectiveness.

WHAT'S UNIQUE ABOUT THIS BOOK

You will find many books about specific quality standards, such as ISO 9000 or Baldrige, or about management approaches like the Balanced Scorecard, or improvement methodologies like Six Sigma. Each of these books tends to promote that particular approach and goes into detail about how to successfully implement it. There are few books that I am aware of that attempt to show how all these different approaches and methodologies might potentially complement each other and form the basis of a new systems approach to management.

By better understanding how these approaches all potentially fit together, managers will be able to use these tools more effectively in a much more integrated approach. It will help companies avoid the "program du jour" management trap of jumping from one of these approaches to the next looking for the ultimate solution, when the best solution may simply be using these individual approaches more effectively *in concert with each other* as part of an integrated systems approach to management.

WHY THIS BOOK IS IMPORTANT

We are at an important crossroads. Within the profession of quality management, I have learned it is important for a good quality manager to stay at least two steps ahead of the rest of the organization in order to provide leadership to keep the organization moving forward. Over the past 5–6 years, however, it has been difficult to figure out what that direction is.

Several years ago, the American Society for Quality Control (ASQC) went through a major transition to become the American Society for Quality (ASQ). That was a significant transition and many people might have thought that would last for an extended period of time, but "quality" as we have known it has already started to move on. Having products that are free of defects is only "table stakes" to play in the game. To be competitive, companies must not only excel at producing products that are free of defects, but also do it at the lowest possible cost and fastest possible cycle time while they specifically match those products against a very dynamic and constantly evolving set of customer needs and expectations.

Successfully meeting these challenges requires a very different approach. It requires broad, cross-functional leadership to develop well-integrated business processes and a more integrated, systems approach to management that optimizes all functions of the business around maximizing customer value to drive business results. Many companies have not recognized the need for this level of integration and new information technology will force businesses to develop and implement this cross-functional approach much faster than they are prepared to deal with it.

Where will this cross-functional leadership come from? Everyone on the senior management team needs to develop more of a cross-functional viewpoint, but an overall leader is typically needed to facilitate this team to further develop and implement this approach. This leader may come from a number of different functional disciplines (information technology, quality management, and others). None of those organizations in most companies is well prepared to take on this role and it will take considerable effort to successfully develop this function.

A ROADMAP FOR USING THIS BOOK

This book has primarily been written for anyone directly involved in:

- Defining and implementing integrated quality and business management systems

- Designing and implementing business processes and any associated systems

- Developing and implementing process improvement methodologies or initiatives

It is intended to provide an overview of the major areas in a system designed for business excellence and how it all fits together to drive business results. It is not intended to be an exhaustive treatment of all areas that might need to be considered, nor does it attempt to duplicate the many excellent works that are available in each of these individual areas. Readers who want to gain a thorough understanding of the areas in the book may want additional information that goes beyond the overview level that is included in the book. A list of additional references, as well as resources and tools for additional help in implementing some of the concepts in this book, can be found at http://www.bizexgroup.com (see Appendix B for additional information). Other readers who want to develop a high-level understanding of the management approach and the concepts behind it to implement more effective business management systems should read the following chapters for a quick overview:

- Chapters 1–3 (Introduction, Background on Quality Standards, and Management Approach)

- Chapters 9–11 (Putting it All Together, Keeping the Progress Moving, and Overall Summary)

A saying I have always liked is, "Quality is a journey. It is not a destination." This book presents a very broad view of how quality is likely to evolve into a broader focus on business excellence.

- Very few companies have fully achieved this vision of fully integrating a focus on quality management with their business objectives.

- All companies are at different stages of maturity in integrating a focus on quality with their business objectives.

- It will take time and perhaps a number of incremental (small or large) steps to achieve this vision.

At the end of the book, a simple assessment tool is provided that can be used to evaluate the maturity of your current management system and to identify and prioritize areas for improvement.

1

Introduction

A new approach to quality management is emerging. Many companies are calling it *business excellence* because the word "quality" typically has a narrower connotation associated with the quality of products and services the company delivers to its customers. Businesses that have successfully implemented a business excellence strategy have made quality an integral part of the way the business is designed. It goes beyond the quality of products and services, and takes on a broader meaning of maximizing the effectiveness of the business in meeting or exceeding customer value expectations and using continuous improvement to drive business results. It is the total quality of how the business operates as a system.

This is not another management fad; in fact, one of the biggest obstacles to successful implementation is overcoming the tendency of many companies to latch on to the next management fad or to implement quality standards and improvement methodologies as a "program." A fundamental shift in thinking is needed to break out of the "program du jour" management trap that has been so popular in the past to successfully implement a business excellence strategy:

- Within the area of quality and business process improvement standards and methodologies, companies say, "We're going to do Six Sigma" (or Baldrige, or ISO 9000, et cetera). Many of these standards have been poorly implemented because few companies take the time to fully understand how to use them as tools for business process improvement and really make them an integral part of their business management system.

- Information technology also suffers from that approach. You hear companies say "We're going to do CRM (customer relationship management)" or "We're going to do knowledge management."

They are often applied as single-dimension solutions to what is a much more complex multidimensional problem and, as a result, many times do not meet expectations. Gartner Group estimates that companies waste as much as 20 percent of the $2.7 trillion spent worldwide annually on technology.[1] New information technology that is rapidly evolving will further compound this problem.

Instead of redefining a business around the latest management approach, quality standard, improvement methodology, or information technology paradigm, we need to think of businesses as complex systems and use well-established systems engineering principles to design and maximize the effectiveness of the system. The various management approaches, quality standards, and information technology capabilities are only tools that should be used appropriately in that context to solve business system problems and a well-integrated, cross-functional approach is needed that considers all aspects of the problem and the solution.

The exact implementation of systems that use quality management principles to achieve business excellence may vary widely among companies and there is no "cookbook" approach as to how to do it. However, there are a number of common elements in most systems designed for business excellence that will be discussed in this book. The design approach is critical—it requires an integrated approach to designing a quality and business management system that is based on an understanding of the company's key business objectives and how the company operates (or should operate) as a system. The approach should also be based on using the most appropriate quality standards, improvement methodologies, and information technology systems as tools in support of the overall design.

HISTORICAL BACKGROUND AND TRENDS

The Evolution of the "Systems" Approach to Quality Management

Following World War II, Dr. W. Edwards Deming and others introduced a new, innovative and integrative approach to achieving quality called *total quality management* (TQM) to Japan. By using TQM, many Japanese firms significantly improved their quality levels, decreased their operating costs, and rapidly increased their domination of world markets.[2]

Probably the most important lesson that can be learned from TQM is that relying primarily on inspection of a product at the output of a production system is a very inefficient and ineffective way to manage quality. A far better approach is to develop an understanding of the processes and other factors within the production system that contribute to the quality of the final product, and *design the production system itself* to reliably and consistently produce products that are free of defects. The idea, of course, is that if the system itself was reliable and verifiable, there would be a much higher level of confidence that the products would be reliable and only a limited amount of final product inspection would be necessary.

When Dr. Deming and others initially began to define the concept of TQM after World War II, they could not possibly have anticipated the different ways that it would be implemented across many different industries for over 50 years. TQM is now more than 50 years old and the basic princi ples behind it are still fundamentally sound; but the complexity of today's business environment, as well as new developments in information technology, creates a very different context:

- In today's rapidly changing environment, managing the quality of products and services that a company produces is no longer sufficient—it does no good to build high quality, defect-free products if customers prefer something entirely different. The challenge today is the very nature of how the business itself is managed to maximize customer value in a rapidly changing environment.

- The gradual, incremental process improvements that have been associated with TQM in the past may not be sufficient for some of the radical change that is needed to address rapidly changing technology and customer values. "One-shot" reengineering efforts that were popular in the late 1980s and early 1990s have also not been sufficient. An integrated approach that is optimized for continuous and ongoing change (incremental as well as radical) is needed.

- The explosive growth of the enterprise resource planning (ERP) systems, the Internet, and worldwide communications is breaking down walls between functional departments, companies, customers, and suppliers. It is requiring that companies integrate not only their own organization, but the complete value chain of which the company is a part also. The rapid evolution of new architectures based on information technology standards will further accelerate this trend.

The organizational structures and approaches for dealing with these issues in most companies have not changed significantly in the last 10–15 years and have been fragmented.

We need to extend the scope of what "quality" means today and redefine the original TQM principles to fit this new context. The key to this is beginning to understand the operation of the entire business as a *system.* The principle is the same as the original principle behind TQM on a much larger scale. Instead of relying primarily on managing the outputs of the business system, we need to focus on how the business system itself is designed to produce the desired output.

The value of treating a business organization as a system is that it helps to break down the complexity and provides a framework for understanding cause-and-effect relationships that go on inside the system. Figure 1.1 is a simplified model that can be used to view a business as a system.

Note: This is only one possible model for viewing a business as a system. It is somewhat general and universal, and is used throughout this book to provide a frame of reference; however, it is not meant to preclude other approaches for viewing the business as a system.

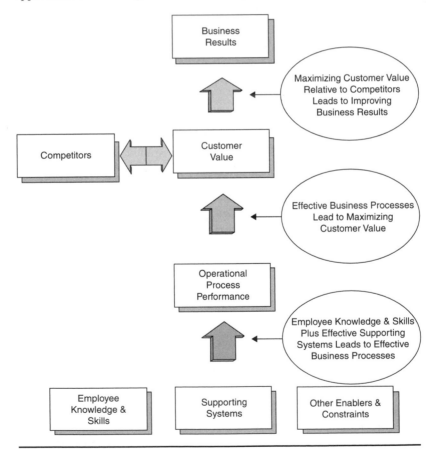

Figure 1.1   Business system model.

Our knowledge and understanding of business systems is still at a very primitive stage. During the late 1980s and 1990s, there has been a lot of experimenting with different approaches for optimizing the performance of business systems; but in many cases, people were looking for a quick solution without attempting to understand the overall system and it's questionable what we've really learned from it.

- Different approaches for quality management and business process improvement have competed with each other and it isn't clear how (and if) they fit together.

- The complexity of these problems is also not well understood, and many times there is an attempt to apply one-dimensional solutions to what is a multifaceted problem.

- Many companies are not putting the time and commitment into the real work that is needed to make these approaches successful and to sustain any positive results.

Quick and simple solutions have limited effectiveness and a one-time reengineering effort will not provide an ongoing solution in itself. The fundamental problem is not that these different tools and approaches are ineffective; we need to rethink the way companies are organized and managed to apply them successfully. Our basic approach to management hasn't changed significantly since the 1980s, and applying any of these approaches for improvement without considering the overall business as a system can be equivalent to doing a major engine overhaul on a Model T Ford. At the end, you wind up with a Model T Ford with a more efficient engine.

"In a global environment where new technologies, mergers, acquisitions, and alliances are creating hyper-competition and market complexity, we find businesses operating now under new rules: Built to last now means built to change; systems integration must include people integration; company leadership now requires ecosystem leadership."

"These new rules require greater alignment among technology, systems, people and organizational units. No longer can a manager attempt to handle 'one thing at a time.' Managers must align all elements so that every function is designed, operated, and managed to enable performance excellence today and rapid adaptation to the changing markets tomorrow."[3]

To meet today's challenges, organizations (large and small) need to be optimized for rapidly adapting to continuous change (both incremental and

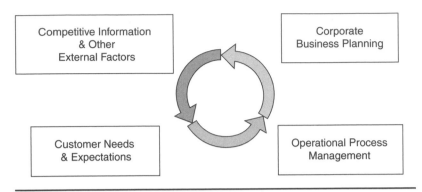

Figure 1.2   Continuous improvement cycle.

radical), as shown in Figure 1.2 (a more detailed version of this planning model is given in chapter 3).

Converging Trends

A number of different approaches to business process improvement, business management, quality management, and information technology are beginning to converge to form the basis of an integrated "systems" approach to management, as shown in Figure 1.3.

Business Process Improvement

During the 1990s, the reengineering movement, which has been associated with more radical process changes, and the total quality management (TQM) movement, which has been associated with more incremental business process improvements, were somewhat competitive. Although these two approaches were potentially complementary, they were rarely integrated.

In the past 10–15 years, Six Sigma has evolved as a methodology for implementing business process improvement initiatives (radical improvements as well as more incremental approaches); however, Six Sigma has been implemented in many cases as a "program" and is not frequently integrated with other approaches to quality management, such as ISO 9000 and Baldrige.

Although the Six Sigma approach is very sound, the potential problem is in how it is implemented. There is a risk that companies will treat Six Sigma as the "program de jour" or the next management "fad" and will not really take the time to understand what role it plays and how it fits into an overall management system that may possibly use other standards, best practices, and methodologies.

Business Management

Business management has typically gone through phases that were dominated by a single discipline. The influence of financial management has dominated management thinking since Alfred Sloan was managing General Motors. The problems in today's world are typically much more complex and demand well-integrated, cross-functional solutions. There is now a growing understanding that customer value really drives financial results and is the most fundamental driving force for integrating these technologies into an overall business management system. It is essentially the key to the "puzzle" of creating a more integrated management environment.

Quality and Quality Management

The concept of quality and quality management has also gone through significant change. Feigenbaum identified a number of significant changes in the direction of quality:[4]

- Quality has gone from emphasis on the reduction of things gone wrong to emphasis on the increase in things gone right for the customer, and subsequent improvement in company sales and revenue growth.

- Quality has moved from the past focus on management of quality to emphasis on the quality of managing, operating, and integrating the marketing, technology, production, information, and finance areas throughout a company's quality value chain with the subsequent favorable impact on manufacturing and service effectiveness.

- Most current quality standards, such as the year 2000 version of the ISO 9000 standard and its variants, require continuous improvement and customer satisfaction rather than the focus on static quality control and reduction of defects that has been common in the past. However, very few companies fully appreciate and implement the fundamental changes that are needed to shift from a compliance orientation to quality management to a broader emphasis on continuous improvement. To develop an effective focus on continuous improvement requires a much higher level of integration with the business strategy to ensure that the improvement initiatives are well integrated and all going in the right direction.

Information Technology

The rapid evolution of enterprise resource planning (ERP) systems has had a very dramatic impact on redefining the role of information systems as an integral and inseparable component of a business process management approach. New technology is rapidly evolving that will significantly extend the notion of an ERP system and encapsulate the entire Internet as a very powerful and tightly interconnected infrastructure to support new ways of doing business.

However, implementation of these systems is increasingly complex, and in many companies there is a very large gap between the people who understand the technology and others who need to contribute to the definition and implementation of an effective, cross-functional solution. The lack of integration between the business and operational requirements, the design and definition of business processes, and the implementation of the information technology available to support those requirements has led to less than optimal results in many cases:

> "Productivity and economic growth soared in the 1990s as companies poured billions into technology to power everything from e-commerce to inventory management. Research now shows companies also waste billions on tech . . . Morgan Stanley estimates that U.S. companies threw away $130 billion in the past two years on unneeded software and other technology . . . worldwide companies waste as much as 20 percent of the $2.7 trillion spent annually on tech, estimates research firm Gartner."[5]

Information technology suffers from the same "program de jour" problems as other management fads. You hear people say, "We're going to do CRM" or "We're going to do knowledge management" in the same way they might say "We're going to do Six Sigma" or "We're going to do TQM." It is a single-dimension solution to a multidimensional problem and the complexity of successfully implementing it is not fully appreciated in many cases.

From a technology perspective, these methodologies have already converged significantly, as shown in Figure 1.3, and the major obstacle to be overcome is organizational rather than technological. Much of the differences in these approaches in actual practice can be attributed to the fact that they are typically driven from different perspectives by people that do not have the full range of knowledge in all of these areas to develop a balanced approach.

- Few companies are well organized to implement these concepts in an integrated approach to management and many may not yet clearly see the underlying systemic requirements that are implied.

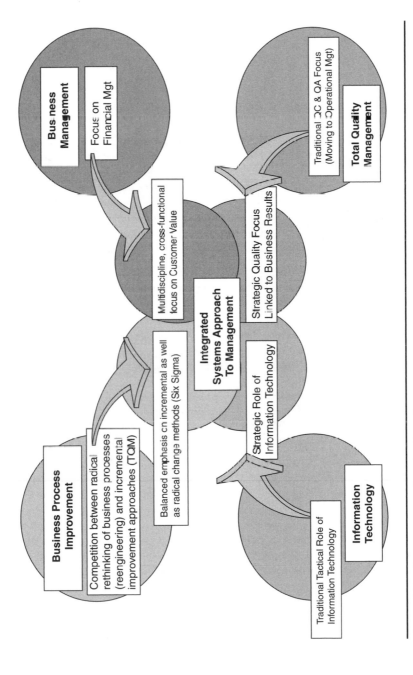

Figure 1.3 Convergence of major trends.

- In today's functionally oriented organizations, there are a limited number of people who have a broad enough cross-functional perspective to see how these approaches potentially fit together and complement each other.

A VISION FOR THE FUTURE

The Importance of Systems Thinking

The results of many total quality management (TQM), strategic information systems, and reengineering efforts during the late 1980s and 1990s have been questionable; in many cases, people have been hopping from one management "fad" to the next looking for a quick solution to complex problems with limited results. "Most companies have been playing 'The Improvement Game,' like contestants on *The Wheel of Fortune.* Management spins the wheel when the current improvement program loses momentum."[6]

> "Americans are our own worst enemy when it comes to new business concepts. We love novelty and newness. We become so enamored with new ideas, we burn through them the way a child rips through toys on Christmas morning—squeals of delight, followed by three or four minutes of interest, then onto the next plaything. That is our pattern with new management techniques, too."[7]

Every time a new management technique comes into vogue, whatever came before it is tossed out and forgotten and the new approach becomes a "paradigm" for redefining how the business is managed. The "Dotcom" era was even worse; during that era, it became common to put together a multimillion dollar business with nothing more than a Web site and some charismatic marketing without any hope of it ever showing a profit. Developing a very fast growth business with little or no foundation became the norm and we essentially "threw out the book" of good management practice that has been built up over many years.

American business is in search of a new paradigm for the future; but a new paradigm is not the answer. It is time to begin synthesizing a body of knowledge of how to apply these various management approaches and quality standards more effectively. What is needed is a completely new approach of looking at business systems from a very broad cross-functional perspective that integrates quality, process improvement/reengineering, and information technology into a systems approach for continuous improvement.

The key to this is systems thinking; it requires developing an understanding of how the business operates (or should operate) as a system and then using whatever standards and best practices are appropriate as a "checklist" of items to consider in making the business operate more effectively.

- Companies who do not use systems thinking tend to redefine their business to follow whatever approach is in vogue. They "mimic" what others do or mechanically implement an approach and do not necessarily fully understand what it means to their business. They say things like "We're going to do Six Sigma," or "Baldrige," or the "Balanced Scorecard," or "Knowledge Management," et cetera. Whatever approach they choose becomes a new "paradigm" for defining how to manage the business and different approaches are typically seen as competitive (how can you choose more than one approach to model your business after?)

- Companies who have a well-established systems perspective of how their business operates see each standard or management approach that comes along from a different perspective. They know and understand how their business operates from a systems perspective and they tend to understand each of these approaches at a deeper level. They understand the principles behind the approach and see how those principles might be used to help improve their business performance. They are able to assimilate multiple approaches easily into their business model because they see them only as tools, not as paradigms to completely redefine how their business is managed.

Adopting this type of "systems thinking" approach for business management has some obvious benefits:

1. Instead of being limited to only one approach, such as Six Sigma, a company can much more easily integrate a number of approaches and best practices that may be relevant to their business.

2. Companies more effectively use each of these individual approaches because:

- They are not limited by one approach and can pick and choose the best management tool for each situation.

- They've taken the time to understand the principles behind each approach and adapted it as needed to the unique needs of their business.

- They have more effectively integrated each individual tool or approach with any other requirements for successful implementation within the context of their business system.

3. Each time a new approach comes along, it is no longer a gut-wrenching change to redefine the whole management system around that particular approach and the learning curve that was gained by whatever approach came before it is not lost.

The implications of implementing this systems thinking approach are broad and far-reaching; it requires rethinking the way business management systems, quality management systems, and information systems are defined and implemented and using a systems engineering approach to create a common understanding of how the overall business management system works and is improved continuously.

Designing Integrated Management Systems

The approach of this book is to define some key principles, it is not a prescriptive approach. Managers designing management systems need to interpret the principles in the context of their business and design an appropriate solution. There are two important principles:

A Business is a Complex System

There are many complex systems that will never be fully understood (the human body is a good example); however, an understanding of how some of the major elements of the system work and interrelate to each other is an essential starting point.

- The organization, like the human body, is a system; to make it healthy you must consider the whole as well as the parts. That requires looking at the "system" from a broad cross-functional perspective, just as in a medical analogy, a general practitioner provides an overall view and integrates a team of other specialists as needed. In the typical organization, very few people have this broad, cross-functional perspective.

- The relationship of the organization to other systems (businesses) in a supply chain is also important to understand. New information technology is rapidly breaking down some of the traditional barriers to effectively sharing information across these boundaries; however, the technology is beginning to move faster than our ability to manage it.

A Systems Approach is Needed
to Effectively Design Business Systems

A systems approach that views the business from a cross-functional perspective is essential for successfully understanding and implementing the concepts in this book. "Quality" must be an integral part of the way the business is designed. It must take on a broader meaning of maximizing the effectiveness of the business in meeting or exceeding customer value expectations and driving business results. It is the total quality of how the business operates as a system.

Many quality standards focus on the criteria and requirements that a system must meet and how it can be audited or assessed against those requirements. There is a much lower level of focus on how to design effective business management systems. A disciplined approach is needed that focuses on the results to be achieved by the system and considers all factors (soft as well as hard) that influence successful accomplishment of those results. The discipline that is needed is essentially a systems engineering approach to designing business systems.

Systems engineering is a discipline that is not new. It has been used for years to design complex systems. It has not been widely applied to the design of business systems in the past because businesses are not typically thought of as complex systems. New information technology is advancing faster than our capability for designing business systems to effectively manage it.

Changes to a system must also be understood from a systems perspective. Failure to fully understand the systems concept can lead to implementation of simple solutions that appear to solve one problem, but have unintended consequences in another area.

The use of these "principles" may vary considerably from one company to the next and nothing in this book is intended to be a prescriptive approach. It is also important to acknowledge that companies are at various stages of maturity in implementing this kind of system. Some companies may already be "pushing the envelope" and have already succeeded in using a systems approach to integrate their business and quality systems. Others may have no quality system at all or an older compliance-oriented ISO 9000 quality management system that is not well oriented with helping to drive business results.

There are four primary areas of focus that need to be addressed to further develop well-integrated management systems designed for business excellence:

Management Approach

Under pressure to streamline their organizations, many companies have resorted heavily to downsizing and laying off people to reduce overhead and to become more efficient. In a number of cases, that has produced results in a relatively short time. Now that that has been done, however, companies are left with the question of "now what do we do?" when quick and simple solutions no longer work.

In many cases, cutting people is also a single-dimensional solution to a multidimensional problem. In order to see these solutions in the right overall perspective, a different approach to management is needed. In particular, we need to reemphasize that viewing the business as a "system" and inspiring "systems thinking" throughout the organization is an essential and fundamental requirement to create an environment that facilitates continuous improvement.

American management is at a crisis point. The "Dotcom" era created a very "fast and free-wheeling" management style. For example, it became common practice to put together a multimillion dollar business in the "Dotcom" era with nothing more than a Web site and some charismatic marketing without any hope of it ever showing a profit. We essentially "threw out the book" of good management practice that has been built up over the years. That has ultimately led to some of the accounting debacles we have today of companies overstating their business results to cover up some of these problems. What is needed is to get back to some of the basics of good management practice that we have lost sight of.

Integrated Management Models
In order to implement a systems approach to management, models are needed to help visualize and understand how the organization operates (or should operate) as a system. This may include:

- Enterprise models that provide a high-level view of the business, vision and mission, key business objectives, and the core processes that define the management structure

- Process maps that show how the processes work at a more detailed level

- Lifecycle models that describe how the organization manages changes that take place over a period of time, such as new product development initiatives

These models provide the framework for defining the management system and integrating whatever quality standards, best practices, and improvement methodologies become an integral part of how the business operates.

Strategic Alignment and Metrics
Process improvement and reengineering efforts in many cases have not been well connected to strategic goals. There is often a relatively weak connection between the people in the organization who understand the business processes, the senior managers who are creating the overall business strategy, and any resources that may be needed for business process improve-

ment and reengineering. Management systems that are based primarily around financial metrics are also proving to be inadequate for effective business management in today's environment.

What is needed is to realign some of the functions in the organization to more effectively integrate these efforts and to create a planning and review process with clearly defined goals and objectives based on customer value. Better metrics are also needed that more clearly provide information on some of the cause-and-effect relationships that drive financial results.

Integrated Process Improvement Methodology

A more integrated approach to process improvement and reengineering is also needed that is well integrated with the management system to ensure that all process improvement initiatives are well-planned, effective, and well-aligned with the goals of the integrated management system.

Six Sigma has emerged as an excellent methodology for managing improvement initiatives; however, Six Sigma is only a tool. It's not, in itself, a management system, and it has capabilities and limitations that need to be understood in the context of the overall management system.

Reengineering is an improvement methodology that may be currently considered to be "out of vogue"; however, there are important lessons that can be learned from it that should not be forgotten. Reengineering teaches us that sometimes it is necessary to step back and take a fresh look at the way things are done. In some cases, it is more appropriate to blow away the process and start over with an entirely different approach. Those opportunities for real breakthrough improvement results might not be discovered from an incremental process-oriented improvement approach like TQM or Six Sigma.

Finally, the impact of information systems cannot be ignored. Very few improvement initiatives have no information systems impact and an integrated approach is needed that blends the design and definition of the business process with the information systems that support it. Existing information technology such as ERP systems has not made that an easy thing to do, but new technology is evolving based on standards that will make an integrated approach much more practical in the future. Few companies are well prepared to deal with the challenge that presents, however.

Figure 1.4 shows how these areas fit with the systems model of a business that was previously discussed. This diagram also shows a "roadmap" of how the chapters in this book fit into this overall model. Readers who wish to gain a quick understanding of the overall concept can skip forward to the last chapter, "Putting it All Together." Readers who want to gain more in-depth knowledge for implementing each of the areas in this model can use this diagram as a "roadmap" to navigate through the sections of the book.

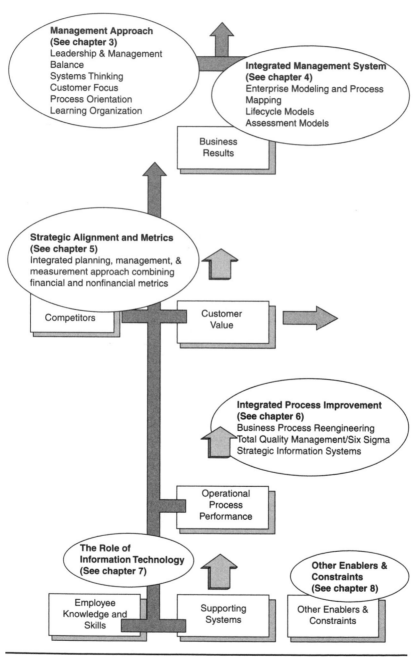

Figure 1.4 Business "system" system model and roadmap.

EXAMPLES OF INTEGRATED MANAGEMENT SYSTEMS

Sprint

Sprint is an example of a company that has created an integrated management system. "Excellence through Quality" is a very important core value at Sprint. Although the quality system does not use a formalized quality certification system such as ISO 9000, Sprint's commitment to quality goes beyond the ISO requirements and is fully engrained in the culture of the company. It is an integral part of their business management system.

The strongest part of the Sprint system is the way they have fully integrated quality into the fabric of the business:

"Sprint Quality Is the Way We Run Our Business"

"To successfully run a business like Sprint, we must do many things well—we must create and communicate a vision from the entire company, establish overarching goals and values, establish and execute business strategies, develop products and services that meet the needs of our customers, hire and train employees, solve day-to-day problems, and more. Sprint Quality addresses how we should accomplish such tasks."[8]

Sprint has created a well-integrated set of goals, essential values, and principles that serve as a unifying theme to integrate everyone in the company and the management system around three key goals:

- Exceptional customer satisfaction

- Inspired, innovative, and empowered employees

- Superior financial results

Cessna Aircraft

Cessna Aircraft is another company that has integrated a focus on quality throughout their business and kept it very well aligned with achieving their business objectives. In fact, Cessna has gone beyond that to integrate quality and their business strategy throughout their whole supply chain. Cessna requires their key growth suppliers to annually perform a Baldrige self-assessment to evaluate areas of strength and weakness. That assessment is then used as the basis of a joint continuous improvement strategy.

Table 1.2 Cessna "High Five" objectives.

"High Five" Strategic Objectives	Supporting Supply Chain Process Strategies
1. **Total customer satisfaction** *We exist as a company to serve our customers.*	• Total Lifecycle Cost Focus • Reliability Improvement • After-Market Support
2. **World quality standard for aviation** *Our customers expect only the best from Cessna.*	• Baldrige Deployment • STARS 2000 & Maturity Path Deployment • Cost of Poor Quality Improvement • Supplier Special Process Control
3. **Breakthrough operating performance** *Improving today's performance to build our future.*	• Integrated Cost Reduction • Enterprise Supply Chain Deployment • Six Sigma/Lean Deployment • Cycle Time and Inventory • Breakthrough Strategies
4. **Top 10 companies to work for in America** *Improving our business results only through engaging our people.*	• Safety • Performance Management Process • Career Development • Employee Training • Communication
5. **Superior financial performance** *Successful companies grow, invest, and generate opportunities.*	• Year-over-year Productivity • Inventory Minimization • Textron Enterprisewide Initiatives • Overhead Management

Cessna's integrated business and quality strategy is based around five key business objectives. Table 1.1 shows how they have integrated their top five business objectives to achieve business excellence throughout their supply chain.[9]

Cessna's management system integrates a number of quality standards and improvement methodologies, including Baldrige, Six Sigma, Lean Manufacturing, and ISO 9000/AS 9000 that are used as tools for ongoing management and improvement.

ENDNOTES

1. J. Hopkins and M. Kessler, "Companies Squander Billions on Tech," *USA Today*, 20 May 2002.
2. "Brief History of Total Quality Management (TQM)," http://leroy.cc.uregina.ca/~urqweb/paage3.html.

3. T. Reichart and J. Tomlinson, "Leading the People-Side," *Executive Excellence* (November 2001): 3.
4. A. Feigenbaum, "Changing Concepts and Management of Quality Worldwide," ASQ *Quality Progress* (December 1997): 47.
5. See note 1.
6. W. Hunicke, "Lessons Learned from the Quality Revolution," *Quality* (May 1994).
7. B. Sheehy, H. Bracey, and R. Frazier, *Winning the Race for Value* (New York: American Management Association, 1996): 104.
8. http://www.sprint.com/sprint/values/quality/.
9. "Cessna Supply Chain Process 2002," provided by Michael Katzorke, Senior Vice President of Supply Chain Management.

2
Quality Standards Background

CHAPTER OVERVIEW

This section is intended as a very basic "primer" for managers who may not be familiar with some of the quality standards (such as ISO 9000) and the improvement methodologies that are discussed in this book. It is a very high-level overview only and is not intended to provide a full and complete understanding of these areas.

Readers should refer to the additional resources provided in Appendix B to supplement the book for more details if necessary. (Experienced quality managers may not need the information in this section.)

ISO 9000

The term *ISO 9000* has two major connotations. One is a specific standard called ISO 9000 *Quality Management Systems—Fundamentals and Vocabulary* and the second connotation is a family of standards that compose the ISO 9000 series related to quality management systems. For example, ANSI/ISO/ASQ Q9001-2000 *Quality Management Systems—Requirements* is actually the specific standard within the ISO 9000 family that defines the specific requirements of the standard. When I use the term *ISO 9000* in this book, I am referring to the family of standards shown in Table 2.1.

ISO 9000 has been a widely recognized international standard in quality management since 1987 and it has several industry-specific derivatives. ISO 9000 was originally developed primarily from a process control perspective. The original version of the standard was based on the premise of "Say what you do, and do what you say"—companies should be very explicit and clear

Table 2.1   ISO 9000 standards family.

Standard	Title
ISO 9000	Quality management systems—Fundamentals and Vocabulary
ISO 9001:1994	Quality systems—Model for quality assurance in design, development, production, installation and servicing (replaced by ISO 9001:2000)
ISO 9002:1994	Quality systems—Model for quality assurance in production, installation and servicing (replaced by ISO 9001:2000)
ISO 9003:1994	Quality systems—Model for quality assurance in final inspection and test (replaced by ISO 9001:2000)
ISO 9001:2000	Quality management systems—Requirements
ISO 9004:2000	Quality management systems—Guidelines for performance improvements

in setting customer's expectations about products and services and develop processes and management systems to ensure that they can meet those requirements predictably and consistently.

General Overview

Historically, one of the key advantages of the ISO 9000 family of standards has been to facilitate international trade. Adopting ISO 9000 as a universal international standard is intended to provide some level of assurance to customers that they can purchase products and services remotely throughout the world with a somewhat consistent level of quality. If I am buying a product from a company in Singapore or Malaysia, how can I be sure the quality of the product is acceptable and the manufacturer will be responsive to resolving any problems that might occur?

Prior to the evolution of the ISO 9000 standard, a company buying the product might mitigate this risk by doing an audit of the potential supplier's facility to determine if the controls were adequate. That type of audit (when the customer directly audits the supplier) is called a *second party audit* in the quality management community. There are several potential problems with that approach:

- It can be very expensive for a buyer to send auditors halfway around the world to inspect a supplier's facility, especially if that company is not a major supplier.

- The supplier potentially would be bombarded with numerous second-party audits from multiple buyers who might have different requirements for quality management. Meeting these multiple requirements would be a confusing and unnecessarily time-consuming process for the suppliers.

- Even if it were feasible to do, there is no guarantee that this kind of approach would be sufficient unless the buyer were to design a complete set of requirements for the supplier's quality management system.

ISO 9000 is meant to be a minimum set of requirements and an ISO 9000 audit is normally a "pass/fail" test. It is a *third-party audit* system; ISO 9000 certification is granted by accredited registrars who perform the auditing to determine if a company meets certification requirements. This third-party auditing and registration approach avoids the above problems that have been associated with second-party auditing:

- It minimizes the need for any individual buyer to directly audit the suppliers; instead, they can rely on the auditing and registration service provided by the third-party registrar.

- The supplier has one consistent set of requirements rather than multiple, potentially conflicting customer requirements and does not have to deal with repetitive audits from multiple sources.

- Having one international standard that everyone agrees on eliminates the need for a buyer to design his or her own requirements and provides a basis for ongoing improvement.

Evolution of the ISO 9000 Standard

Over the years, quality and quality management systems have evolved through a number of generations and the ISO 9000 standard has been revised to follow that evolution as shown in Table 2.2.

The 1994 version of the ISO 9000 standard provided a foundation for building fundamental process management systems; it required some basic process controls to manage the performance of processes, but it didn't significantly address customer value or other operational metrics that might have a critical impact on business effectiveness and, ultimately, on business results. The year 2000 version of the ISO 9000 standard has closed that gap and now includes requirements for customer satisfaction and continuous improvement.

Table 2.2   Evolution of ISO 9000 standard.

Generation	Emphasis	ISO 9000 Revision
"Quality Control"	Emphasizes reduction of defects through inspection and correction	1987
"Quality Assurance Systems"	Emphasizes designing and developing processes that are oriented toward prevention of defects	1994
"Quality Management Systems"	Quality assurance approach plus management system to provide corrective action designed for continuous improvement	2000
"Fully Integrated Business Systems"	The notion of quality takes on a broader context of maximizing customer value to drive business results and is an integral part of the way the business is managed.	Baldrige (not in ISO)

The year 2000 version of the standard also creates more of a systems perspective by better integrating a number of related requirements. For example, in the 1994 version of the standard, the requirements for design of products, manufacturing of products, and servicing of products were all in different areas of the standard. In the year 2000 version of the standard, they are all grouped together in a single, more integrated area called "Product Realization."

There is also a new standard, ANSI/ISO/ASQ Q9004-2000 *Quality Management Systems—Guidelines for Performance Improvement,* which is designed to accompany the ISO 9000 standard and provides guidance on how to implement quality management systems for ongoing improvement.

Both of these standards have gone a long way to shifting the emphasis from a compliance orientation to a customer-focused, continuous improvement orientation; however, the real test will be in how the new ISO 9001:2000 standard is implemented in actual practice. It can be a very major shift in thinking to move from the compliance orientation of the 1994 standard to the continuous improvement orientation of the year 2000 version of the standard. It cannot be done effectively in many cases without major rethinking of how the standard has been implemented.

The year 2000 version of the ISO 9000 standard still does not completely make the connection to business results as the Baldrige standard does. There is nothing in ISO 9000 that says a company has to be profitable or successful from a business perspective. That is still a major difference between ISO 9000 and Baldrige—Baldrige does make that connection.

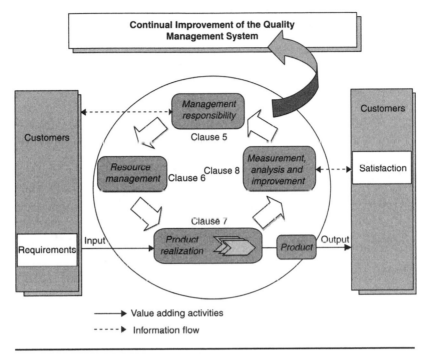

Figure 2.1 ISO 9001:2000 overview.

Source: Adapted from ANSI/TSO/ASQ Q 9001-2000. Used by permission.

The Year 2000 Version of the ISO 9000 Standard

There are five major elements in the current (year 2000) version of the ISO 9000 standard. One major improvement over the 1994 version of the ISO 9000 standard is that it simplified the number of elements and created more of a "systems" view of how the requirements fit together, as shown in Figure 2.1.

Condensing the previous 20 elements of the 1994 version of the ISO 9000 standard and organizing them as shown in Figure 2.1 is intended to help develop the kind of systems thinking approach that is described in this book. One of the criticisms of the 1994 version of the standard was that it led to "tunnel vision." People were overly consumed with details inside each of the 20 elements which were not well integrated and, in some cases, failed to see the big picture of how it all fits together to improve operational effectiveness.

Table 2.3 is a brief description of each of the major clauses of the ISO 9001:2000 standard.

Table 2.3   Elements of the ISO 9001:2000 standard.

Section	Title	Description
4	**Quality management system**	Provides general requirements for the quality management system and defines documentation requirements
5	**Management responsibility**	Defines the requirements top managers must perform to ensure the effectiveness of the quality management system. It includes specific requirements for: • Management commitment • Customer focus • Quality policy • Planning • Responsibility, authority, and communication • Management review
6	**Resource management**	Defines the requirements companies must meet to provide adequate resources to implement and maintain the quality management system and to continually improve its effectiveness. It includes specific requirements for: • Provision of resources • Human resources (including competence and training) • Infrastructure • Work environment
7	**Product realization**	Defines requirements for processes related to product realization. It includes specific requirements for: • Planning of product realization • Customer-related processes • Design and development • Purchasing • Production and service provision • Control of monitoring and measuring devices
8	**Measuring, analysis and improvement**	Defines requirements for monitoring, measuring, analysis, and improvement processes needed to demonstrate conformity of the product, ensure conformity of the quality management system, and continually improve the effectiveness of the quality management system. It includes specific requirements for: • Monitoring and measurement • Control of nonconforming product • Analysis of data • Improvement

Source: adapted from ANSI/ISO/ASQ Q 9001-2000. Used with permission.

The year 2000 version of the ISO 9000 standard is based on the following principles:

- Customer-focused Organization

- Leadership

- Involvement of People

- Process Approach

- Systems Approach to Management

- Continual Improvement

- Factual Approach to Decision Making

- Mutually Beneficial Supplier Relationships

Industry-specific ISO 9000 Variations

Industry-specific quality standards that combine some of the fundamental requirements of ISO 9000 with other more specific criteria in the context of a specific industry have evolved in several major industries:

- QS-9000 is an example that has been widely adopted throughout the automotive industry (it is now being converted to TS-16949).

- AS-9000 has been adopted in the aerospace industry.

- TL 9000 has been developed for the telecommunications industry.

- Consideration is being given to create a new standard based on ISO 9000 for the financial services industry.

All of these standards use the ISO 9000 requirements as a foundation and a base and add additional interpretations of the standard and unique requirements that are appropriate to that industry.

MALCOLM BALDRIGE CRITERIA FOR PERFORMANCE EXCELLENCE

The Malcolm Baldrige criteria are not really a standard in the same sense that ISO 9000 is a standard. It has some of the characteristics of a standard:

- It is administered by NIST (National Institute of Standards and Technology), which is an agency of the National Bureau of Standards.

- It is annually reviewed and revised to reflect best practices and published as a controlled document.

However, it is not enforced like the ISO standard and is not as prescriptive about what has to be done to meet the Baldrige criteria or how to do it.

The Malcolm Baldrige National Quality Award was originally developed to improve competitiveness of U.S. industry through a competitive evaluation and award process. A Baldrige assessment is based on a continuous improvement model and is not a "pass/fail" test. At the conclusion of the assessment, the company will receive an overall score ranging from 0–1000 points indicating how effectively their business system implements the Baldrige criteria.

It is also based on a "systems view" of the business and approaches it from the top-down perspective, with a strong emphasis on customer satisfaction and business performance, as shown in Figure 2.2.

Table 2.4 is a brief summary of the criteria in the 2003 Baldrige standard.

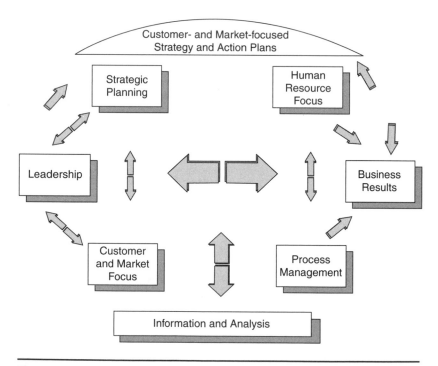

Figure 2.2   2003 Baldrige criteria—A systems perspective.

Malcolm Baldrige National Quality Award. 2003 Baldrige Criteria for Performance Excellence.

Table 2.4 Summary of 2003 Baldrige criteria.[1]

Criteria	Description	Point Value
Leadership	"Examines how your organization's senior leaders set and address values, directions, and performance expectations, as well as a focus on customers and other stakeholders, empowerment, innovation, and learning. Also examined is how your organization addresses its responsibilities to the public and supports key communities."	120
Strategic planning	"Examines how your organization develops strategic objectives and action plans. Also examined are how your chosen strategic objectives and action plans are deployed and how progress is measured."	85
Customer and market focus	"Examines how your organization determines requirements, expectations, and preferences of customers and markets. Also examined is how your organization builds relationships with customers and determines the key factors that lead to customer acquisition, satisfaction, and retention and to business expansion."	85
Information and analysis	"Examines your organization's information management and performance measurement systems and how your organization analyzes performance data and information."	90
Human resource focus	"Examines how your organization motivates and enables employees to develop and utilize their full potential in alignment with your organization's overall objectives and action plans. Also examined are your organization's efforts to build and maintain a work environment and an employee support climate conducive to performance excellence and to personal and organizational growth."	85
Process management	"Examines the key aspects of your organization's process management, including customer-focused design, product and service delivery, and key business and support processes. This category encompasses all key processes and all work units."	85
Business results	"Examines your organization's performance and improvement in key business areas—customer satisfaction, product and service performance, financial and marketplace performance, human resources results, and operational performance. Also examined are performance levels relative to those of competitors."	450

COMPARISON OF
ISO 9000 AND BALDRIGE

Figure 2.3 shows how the Baldrige and ISO 9000 standards fit into the business system model that will be used in this book. The Baldrige criteria emphasize having a clearly defined business strategy based on customer value and connecting that to all aspects of the company required to achieve those objectives, but does not go too far into detail about how to effectively implement process controls. Baldrige is a sophisticated and much more comprehensive model than ISO 9000 and is not as prescriptive in many respects. Table 2.5 shows a summary of several key points of comparison.

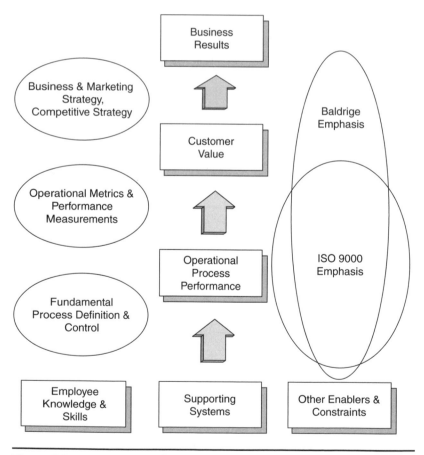

Figure 2.3   Comparison of ISO 9000 and Baldrige standards.

Table 2.5   Comparison of ISO 9000 and Baldrige standards.

Comparison	ISO 9000	Baldrige
Primary emphasis	Process control (year 2000 standard adds continuous improvement and customer satisfaction)	"TQM" style approach to maximize effectiveness and competitiveness
Scope	International	United States (similar efforts becoming adopted internationally)
Type of criteria	"Pass/Fail" audit (compliance orientation)	Business effectiveness assessment (continuous improvement orientation)
Evaluation criteria	Fairly objective	More subjective
Strengths	Strong emphasis on process control, international standardization, and acceptance	Alignment with business goals is broader; TQM emphasis

A Baldrige assessment typically starts at the top of a company, explores their business objectives, and looks "vertically" into the company at the alignment of all elements of the business system with achieving those objectives. An ISO 9000 audit is typically more of a "horizontal" approach of examining processes in a company to see if they are effectively designed and implemented to meet the requirements of the ISO standard.

Process control, which is the primary focus of ISO 9000, is only one element of the Baldrige framework, and the Baldrige criteria are not as prescriptive about process requirements. Baldrige also includes three major areas that are not part of the ISO standard:

- Strategic planning

- Leadership

- Business results

Many state-level quality programs have been developed with the same or similar criteria to the National Baldrige Criteria for Performance Excellence. One of the problems with the Baldrige Award, as with ISO 9000 in many cases, is that it has been implemented as a "quality program." When it was originally implemented as a quality award, companies entered the competition to win the award; and in a number of cases, that effort was not sustained.

Interest in competing for the Baldrige Award has diminished somewhat over the years; however, many companies are recognizing that the Baldrige criteria are a very useful framework for evaluating the maturity and effectiveness of their management system. Companies are using the criteria as a tool for self-assessment, regardless of whether they actually compete for the award or not.

COMPLIANCE VS. CONTINUOUS IMPROVEMENT STANDARDS

ISO 9000 has developed a bad reputation because it has been poorly implemented in many cases. Because it is a mandatory requirement to do business in some industries, companies sometimes go through the mechanics of implementing the requirements so that they can claim ISO certification. In some of these cases, the implementation is superficial and companies do not take the time to understand how the fundamental requirements can be integrated into an overall management system to improve the company's business and operational effectiveness. *The fault in many of these cases is not with the standard itself—it is in the implementation.*

There is a fundamental difficulty with any standard that requires mandatory compliance and is subject to auditing. It creates an environment where the auditors are seen as the "quality police" to enforce the requirements. I have always strongly believed that "real quality comes from the heart . . . it comes from people who believe in what they're doing and take pride in doing it well." When I was a quality manager at Motorola, my manager used to tell me, "Our job is to teach, coach, and audit (in that order)." A good quality manager is a "missionary"; he/she helps others understand how improving quality will increase customer satisfaction and improve the business, coaches them in how to do it well, and "institutionalizes" it as a standard practice throughout the organization.

That is exactly the approach that is needed to implement effective systems designed for continuous improvement. The routine, day-to-day, tactical, compliance-oriented quality control issues should be fully integrated into the operational fabric of the organization and happen "automatically." That frees up the quality management function to assume a more value-added role and act as a process consultant and project manager to drive very proactive process improvement initiatives.

The year 2000 version of the ISO 9000 standard has closed the gap between ISO and Baldrige by requiring continuous improvement and customer satisfaction in addition to the basic compliance requirements. However, the level of effort required to shift from a compliance orientation to a continuous improvement orientation is not well understood by many people implementing the new year 2000 requirements. It can be a significant cultural change and requires a fundamental shift in thinking, as well as a different and more integrated management approach in many cases.

Numerous quality magazines contain advertisements for "quick and easy" conversions to the year 2000 version of the ISO 9000 standard. In many cases, this only applies a thin "veneer" to create the appearance of continuous improvement orientation over a poorly implemented ISO quality management system and perpetuates the problems that have been prevalent with the 1994 version of the ISO 9000 standard.

Because ISO 9000 has been so poorly implemented in the past in many cases, it really requires a complete rethinking of the way quality management systems are implemented to shift from a compliance orientation to a continuous improvement orientation. Companies have not taken the time to understand how these standards can be used as a tool to help create high-performance, customer-focused businesses that are oriented around driving business results and continuous improvement. That is exactly what this book is focused on.

ENDNOTE

1. Malcolm Baldrige National Quality Award, *2003 Criteria for Performance Excellence* (2003).

3

Management Approach

CHAPTER OVERVIEW

Developing a management approach and an organizational environment that supports ongoing continuous improvement is one of the most fundamental requirements for development of a system designed for business excellence.

This chapter summarizes some key management principles that are essential to the successful implementation of most quality and business excellence requirements. Without a commitment to these principles as a foundation, it will be very difficult, if not impossible, to develop a high level of excellence.

The ANSI/ISO/ASQ Q9004-2000 standard, *Quality management systems—Guidelines for performance improvement* identifies a number of very fundamental principles that are essential to the effective implementation of any management system, including the year 2000 version of the ISO 9000 standard, Six Sigma, and Baldrige:[1]

- Customer-focused organization

- Leadership

- Involvement of people

- Process approach

- Systems approach to management

- Continual improvement

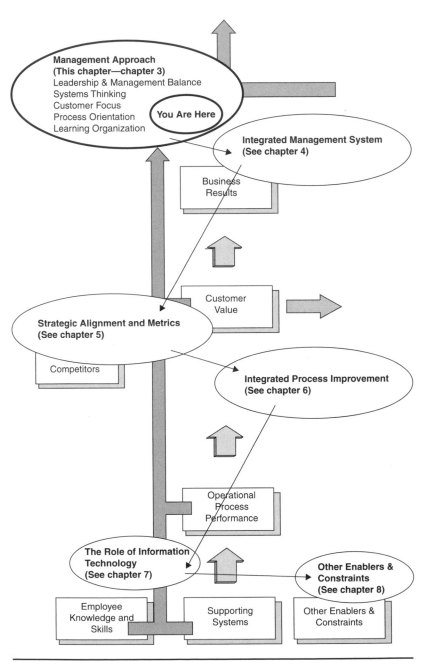

This navigational roadmap is intended to help readers understand the flow of information in these chapters and see how various topics fit into the overall model.

- Factual approach to decision making

- Mutually beneficial supplier relationships

These eight principles are also critical to implement the systems approach to management and business excellence focus that is described in this book. A number of fundamental shifts in thinking are also required to adopt and implement a more integrated approach to management:

1. Leadership and management balance

2. Shift to a customer focus

3. Shift to a process-centered orientation

4. Shift to a systems thinking approach

5. Creating a learning organization environment

LEADERSHIP AND MANAGEMENT BALANCE

Most authors distinguish *leadership* from *management.* Traditional management teaching:[2]

- Implies that the ideal organization is orderly and stable and that organizational process can and should be engineered so that things run like clockwork

- Focuses attention on short-term results

- Teaches that managers should be cool and analytical and separate emotion from work

- Suggests that the job of management is primarily one of control: the control of resources, including time, money, materials, and people

The Leadership Challenge[3] notes that leaders,

". . . had visions and dreams of what could be. They had absolute and total personal belief in those dreams, and they were confident in their abilities to make extraordinary things happen . . . In some ways leaders live their lives backward. They see pictures in their mind's eye of what the results will look like even before they've started their project, much as an architect draws a blueprint or an engineer builds a model. Their clear image of the future pulls them forward . . . Leaders breathe life into the hopes and dreams of others and enable them to see the exciting possibilities that the future holds. Leaders forge a unity of purpose by showing constituents how the dream is for the common good."

Both a short-term, tactical management orientation and a broader, strategic, leadership orientation are essential; however, leadership is becoming particularly important in today's business environment, as companies need to dynamically and rapidly adjust to changes in their business environment:

- The events of September 11th in the United States have had a dramatic impact on our way of life and the economy, and we are slowly recovering from that. Financial accounting scandals, such as Enron and WorldCom, and other similar events have called into question the integrity of many fundamental business and organizational practices that are at the heart of our economic vitality and way of living.

- Many people are feeling battered from the impact of all of this and strong leadership is absolutely essential to lead us into the future. We have been lulled into a false sense of security by putting too much faith in institutions and business practices, and we have lost site of the vital role leadership and integrity play in any business.

There are a number of lessons that can be learned from this:

- Institutions without strong leadership and high levels of integrity have a very uncertain future and a concerted effort is needed to refocus those values to restore public confidence in American business.

- There is a need to continuously and critically examine our business practices to discover this kind of weakness before it develops into such a crisis.

Good to Great by Jim Collins is based on extensive research into companies that have successfully made the transition from a good company to a great company and sustained being a great company for at least 15 years. The book identifies the leadership role as one of the most important factors that differentiates these companies from similar companies in the same industry that failed to reach or sustain "great" performance. The book identifies five levels of leadership.[4] The highest level is a "level 5 leader which is someone who 'Builds enduring greatness through a paradoxical blend of personal humility and professional will.' "

One of the great leaders that significantly inspired me was Martin Luther King. In my opinion, he is a good example of a "Level 5 Executive." I have read his "I Have a Dream" speech from the 1960s many times.[5] What made Martin Luther King such a great leader is exactly the "paradoxical blend of personal humility and professional will" that Jim Collins defines as a "Level 5 Executive." Abraham Lincoln had some of the same characteristics of humility mixed with a broad vision of the future to which he was deeply committed. Both very powerfully stated a vision for the future that had significant and lasting impacts, and backed it up with a very high level of personal integrity and commitment. Compare that to others in the civil rights movement who have a higher level of personal gain and recognition as a motivator and are more focused on quick, short-term results, and the difference is obvious.

Many of the problems that we see in today's environment—such as the accounting scandals—can be attributed to intense pressure on achieving short-term results in a very difficult economy combined with self-motivated executives at the top who are more interested in personal gain than in the long-term success of the company.

We are also still suffering from the culture that was predominant in the "Dotcom" era during the 1990s where it was routine for businesses to overstate their business potential and very fast-moving, rapid growth businesses were the norm.

- In that environment, it became commonplace for companies to ignore many of the fundamental principles of good business management and attempt to build a major, fast-growth business on a very weak foundation.

- In those days, there was an illusion that you could easily build a $100 million business on a Web site and some marketing hype as long as it included ".com" somewhere.

A number of lessons can be learned from the "Dotcom" era. On the positive side, it taught us the value of the Internet as an important mechanism for e-commerce and the power it can provide for developing new business ventures very quickly that have broad and far-reaching impact. On the other hand, however, it essentially caused us to throw out the book of good management practice that has been built up over many years.

The vision of the future that is presented in this book is also a long-term vision. Implementing a more integrated systems approach to management described in this book is not something that can be done over night and it is not easy to do. It requires long-term commitment, which requires leadership and vision, but the time is right for businesses to step back and relearn some of the fundamentals of good business management practice that were sometimes thrown out during the "Dotcom" era.

An Example—Sprint

Sprint is an example of a company that has integrated a focus on quality customer satisfaction into its leadership at a number of different levels. The following are some quotes from Sprint managers that are reproduced with permission from Sprint:[6]

> "Sprint Quality provides straightforward and powerful tools that allow me to lead in a fact-based manner. They help me make effective, impactful decisions. The principles of Sprint Quality, combined with the Sprint dimensions found in LINK, have allowed me to improve and increase my leadership skills.
>
> "Sprint Quality is the foundation for the way we conduct ourselves and the way we represent Sprint to our customers. It differentiates us from our competitors and gives Sprint a distinct competitive advantage. Because actions speak louder than words, I do my best to model Sprint Quality. Consistent results and continuous improvement are the best indicators of success. They provide the most compelling reasons for using Sprint Quality."
>
> —Sandy Price, VP HR Development

> "When Sprint Quality was launched more than 10 years ago, I was trained in the tools and techniques and eventually trained others. I quickly learned how powerful Sprint Quality could be in managing daily activities, in improving the profitability of the business, and in ensuring customer satisfaction. I'm absolutely convinced that my achievements and successes are directly attributable to using Sprint Quality to manage my day-to-day work.
>
> "Consistently practicing Sprint Quality creates a culture where people have the freedom to solve cross-functional issues in a fact-based, no fear, and personally rewarding environment. Employees are now empowered to see that they're part of an integrated process . . . one that can be continuously improved through the use of simple, logical and measurable approaches."
>
> —Mike Bray, AVP Finance GMG

> "To me, Sprint Quality is an attitude, a mindset. When you embrace it, you're committing to a level of personal and organizational excellence that insists you add value every day, delight customers, and beat the heck out of the competition. Success—especially long-term success—doesn't happen by accident. Our quality tools help us make better decisions and provide lasting solutions.

"I'm always amazed how well-known Sprint Quality is in our communities. We have more than 200 Sprint associates serving on various nonprofit boards, and many of them have applied the quality tools—especially the concepts for better meetings. As a result, Sprint Quality is having a positive impact beyond our company's walls and directly into the lives of the people we serve."

—Dave Thomas, AVP Corporate Relations & Exec. Director—Sprint Foundation

SHIFT TO A CUSTOMER-FOCUS

What does shifting to a customer focus mean? Most companies would say that they already are customer focused. In fact, very few companies would say they are not, but the real test is how business results are measured. At a minimum, companies that are really committed to a customer focus have integrated traditional financial metrics with nonfinancial metrics that are directly related to customer value to measure their overall business performance. Beyond that, the whole culture of the company, including how business planning is done and how individual performance is measured and rewarded, needs to be aligned with those values.

American business is deeply rooted in financial metrics and many senior executives would say that the primary mission of the company is to create shareholder value.[7] The major flaws in this approach are twofold:

1. As Michael Hammer points out, "Stating that a company's mission is to create shareholder value is ultimately useless because it offers no guide for action. It avoids the question, 'All right, what do we do now?' Whether you're the CEO, a manager, or an employee on the line, if I tell you that your goal is to create wealth for shareholders, I've told you absolutely nothing useful. If, however, we agree that your mission is to create customer satisfaction, you can actually do something. You can begin by looking around for people who want something (even if they don't know it yet) and then find ways to give it to them. In short, creating customer value is a purpose that yields a guide to action. Creating shareholder value yields nothing but questions."[8]

2. There are many limitations in purely financial metrics, as indicated in *The Balanced Scorecard*: "Financial measures are inadequate for guiding and evaluating organizations' trajectories through competitive environments. They are lagging indicators that fail to capture much of the value

that has been created or destroyed by managers' actions in the most recent accounting period. The financial measures tell some, but not all, of the story about past actions and they fail to provide adequate guidance for the actions to be taken today and the day after to create future financial value."[9]

Making the shift from a traditional financial perspective to a customer-focused perspective requires a "giant leap of faith" to believe that if the company does the right things to maximize customer value, the financial results will follow. No company can operate without financial goals and metrics, and the right solution is an integrated set of both financial and nonfinancial metrics, but the critical fundamental shift in thinking is to accept that creation of customer value is the *primary* driver of business results.

The Role of Customer Value

Customer value is an often-misunderstood term. It is usually confused with customer satisfaction. Customer value defines what is important to customers and directly influences their behavior, which ultimately drives business results such as:

- A decision to purchase or repurchase an item

- A recommendation of the company's products and services to others

Customer satisfaction is the result that is achieved when there is an alignment between the value proposition a company offers, what their customers consider to be important, and the company successfully meeting those expectations. There are two components to successfully achieving customer satisfaction results:

1. Picking the right value proposition to align with a target customer segment

Attempting to open a store with a Niemann Marcus approach targeted at customers who are used to shopping at Wal-Mart is going to result in a misalignment. Customers who value low-priced products may not appreciate the value proposition that Niemann Marcus offers.

2. Successfully delivering the value to customer's expectations

Once a company's value proposition has been designed to align with a set of target customer values, the next step is successfully executing and delivering the required value.

The first step of clearly defining customer values and aligning the company's value proposition with those values is a step that is often overlooked. Sometimes companies think they know what is important to customers, wind up measuring something that is irrelevant or unimportant, and overlook other things that are much more important. It requires a close relationship to the customers to understand what is important to them.

Value Disciplines

The importance of using customer value as a primary focus of strategic planning and as one of the key measurements of results (see chapter 4) is becoming critical to gain a sustainable competitive advantage. As Treacy has recognized in *The Discipline of Market Leaders*:

> ". . . no company can succeed today by trying to be all things to all people. It must instead find the unique value that it alone can deliver to a chosen market . . . One point deserves emphasis: Choosing to pursue a value discipline is a central act that shapes every subsequent plan and decision a company makes, which colors the entire organization from its competencies to its culture. The choice of value discipline, in effect, defines what a company does and therefore what it is."[10]

The message of *The Discipline of Market Leaders* is that no company can succeed today by trying to be all things to all people. It must instead find the unique value that it alone can deliver to a chosen market. Three distinct value disciplines have been defined by Treacy—the principle is that companies need to at least be sufficient in all three of them but choose one to excel in as its competitive differentiation:

1. Operational Excellence

"Companies that pursue this [discipline] are not primarily product or service innovators, nor do they cultivate deep, one-on-one relationships with their customers. Instead, operationally excellent companies provide middle-of-the-market products at the best price with the least inconvenience. Their proposition to customers is simple: low price and hassle-free service. Wal-Mart epitomizes this kind of company, with its no-frills approach to mass-market retailing."[11]

2. Product Leadership

"The second value discipline we call product leadership. Its practitioners concentrate on offering products that push performance boundaries.

Their proposition to customers is an offer of the best product, period. Moreover, product leaders don't build their positions with just one innovation; they continue to innovate year after year, product cycle after product cycle. Intel, for instance, is a product leader in computer chips. Nike is a leader in athletic footwear. For these and other product leaders, competition is not about price; it's about product performance."[12]

3. Customer Intimacy

"The third value discipline we have named customer intimacy. Its adherents focus on delivering not what the market wants but what specific customers want. Customer-intimate companies do not pursue one-time transactions; they cultivate relationships. They specialize in satisfying unique needs, which often they, by virtue of their close relationship with—and intimate knowledge of—the customer, recognize. Their proposition to the customer: We have the best solution for you—and we provide all the support you need to achieve optimum results and/or value from whatever products you buy. Ritz Carlton Hotels is an example of a company that excels at customer intimacy."[13]

The value discipline that is chosen as the primary competitive differentiator tends to define the whole company and its culture. For example:

- A company whose primary value discipline is product leadership needs to create an environment which stimulates creative thought. These companies are typically dominated by engineers who might wear jeans and sweatshirts to work.

- In an operational excellence environment, there is a lot less room for creativity. At McDonalds, there is only one way to cook the hamburgers and creativity in how they are cooked is certainly not encouraged. They do the same thing repeatedly at a low cost; that is what operational excellence is and it is reflected in their culture. People wear uniforms to work and are heavily trained in doing things the same way all the time.

I am continually surprised at the number of companies that do not have a clear idea of what customer value discipline they are attempting to maximize. A misalignment between the primary value discipline a company chooses to pursue and its culture is probably not going to yield optimal results. The same engineers in jeans and sweatshirts who were extremely successful in creating new products at the product leadership company are not likely to be as successful at Ritz Carlton Hotels where the primary value discipline is customer intimacy.

Obviously, different customers have different values, and customer segmentation is important for a company to really be customer focused and maximize the alignment of its own value proposition with particular customer values. A very good example of a company who has segmented its customer base is Marriott Hotels. Years ago, there was only one kind of Marriott Hotel. It was the typical "high-end" luxury hotel that Marriott was famous for at one time. Marriott recognized that their customers had different values:

- Some customers valued luxury (liked the covers turned down at night with a piece of chocolate placed on the night table by the bed and were willing to pay a premium price for it). The traditional Marriott Hotel fit this value proposition well.

- Other business travelers were more cost conscious and less concerned about some of these "frills." Convenience of getting in and out and staying in a nice, comfortable room with the right amenities for business travelers was what was important to them. Marriott Courtyard was developed to fit this need.

- Still other cost-conscious families on a budget wanted a low-cost room and amenities that were designed for a family with children, and Fairfield Inns were created to fill that need.

- If Marriott had continued to offer a "one size fits all" approach, they would have missed the mark in satisfying some of these customers because there would have been a misalignment of their value proposition with what that particular customer segment considered important. This strategy has obviously worked well, as other hotel chains—like Hilton—have also followed this approach.

The ultimate level of customer segmentation, of course, is to be able to uniquely tailor your products and services to *individual* consumer needs. In today's world, customer relationship management (CRM) systems have helped companies attempt to achieve that goal. As an example, when I go to Amazon.com to shop for books, I have an account there and it knows who I am, it knows a history of the kinds of products I have purchased in the past, and it proactively suggests similar products that I might be interested in.

Maintaining a customer focus in today's environment—when companies have gone through severe downsizing that has reduced customer service staff—is especially difficult and requires innovative approaches to help manage customer relationships with reduced resources. That is one of the key reasons why customer relationship management (CRM) software has been so popular in recent years. However, CRM is yet another example of an initiative that failed in many situations to yield expected results, because all of the aspects of completely implementing it and making it successful from a business systems perspective were not fully understood.

SHIFT TO A PROCESS-CENTERED ORIENTATION

The company's business processes are what create customer value and achieving superior customer value requires superior business processes, yet many organizations are optimized to achieve functional excellence rather than overall process excellence. As Michael Hammer points out:

> "If our purpose is to create value and processes do that, then better processes will do it better. However, this principle also runs counter to the beliefs of most managers."[14]

As Treacy points out, "What is needed is a thorough renovation of the machinery that creates value—the operating model—so that management can establish leadership in the dimensions of value that it has chosen to offer customers."[15]

Adopting a process orientation can mean a range of things:

- At a minimum, it means that companies should invest in defining what their critical business processes are so that they are aware of the tasks and functions that make up those processes and adopt appropriate metrics to characterize their performance.

- A more complete approach would be to realign the entire company and organizational responsibilities around a process orientation. However, I am aware of few companies that have completely shifted to a total process orientation from a more traditional functionally oriented structure.

Davenport notes that the right solution is probably somewhere in between these extremes:

> "We do not recommend that processes become the only basis for organizational structure. Functional skills are important to a process orientation, as is concern for product management and the running of strategic business units.

"Most firms are well advised to adopt a multidimensional matrix structure, with process responsibility as a key dimension. An organization that wishes to benefit from a process perspective must be prepared to tolerate the well-known problems with matrix structures, including diffusion of responsibility, unclear reporting relationships, and excessive time spent in coordination activities and meetings."[16]

The most important point is that, regardless of how the organization is structured, *process thinking* should permeate the entire company as a predominant way of managing the business. As Michael Hammer points out:

"In the process-centered organization, this program of process improvement is not a secondary and peripheral activity. It is the essence of management. The process-centered organization embodies the notion that one manages a business not by managing budgets, departments, or people, but by managing processes."[17]

It is important to recognize that shifting to a "process-centered" orientation does not mean that the business has to become rigid and inflexible and locked in to a particular way of doing things. During the "Dotcom" era, I worked with a number of fast-moving companies who would say something like, "We don't have time to define our processes, because the business is changing too rapidly and defining our processes will lock us into a particular way of doing things that will make it difficult to change in the future." That is not necessarily the case; there are numerous ways to provide an appropriate level of flexibility in a process and any process should be somewhat dynamic and continuously reviewed for its effectiveness.

An example of a company that has successfully made the transition from a pure functional orientation to a more process-orientated management approach is Cessna Aircraft. The Cessna business process model is shown in Figure 3.1. "In the model, a senior VP owns and leads each of the core processes, and also serves on Cessna's senior leadership team . . . The model itself provided an important step in driving supply chain management into Cessna's corporate culture. The need was to manage processes rather than functions, while at the same time maintaining the specialized expertise needed for leadership of the business and measurement of the processes."[18]

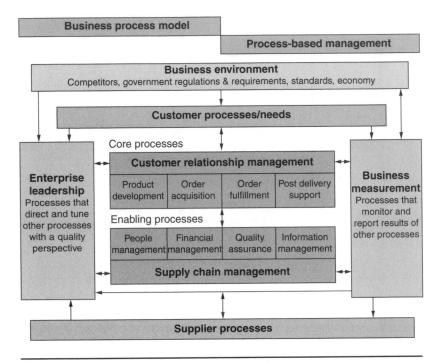

Figure 3.1   Cessna business process model.

SHIFT TO A SYSTEMS THINKING APPROACH

A couple of definitions of the word *system* apply to this context:

- "A group of interacting elements functioning as a complex whole"[19]

- "A complex unity formed of many often diverse parts subject to a common plan or serving a common purpose"[20]

Business organizations have not been typically viewed in this perspective. More often, they are thought of in terms of the traditional organizational hierarchical structure.

Managing an organization structure that is process oriented and in which all processes work together to provide superior customer value requires developing a "systems thinking" approach. Peter Senge describes systems thinking as, "A discipline for seeing wholes . . . a framework for seeing interrelationships rather than things, for seeing patterns of change rather than static snapshots . . . [and] for seeing the structures that underlie complex situations."[21]

George and Weimershirch have also accurately described the role of systems thinking in business performance in their book, *Total Quality Management:*

> "The new management model is nothing more than a discipline for seeing your entire organization, the interrelationships among people and processes that determine success, and the patterns of change that demand vigilance. In an increasingly competitive marketplace, you cannot hope to survive in a system that is out of control. And it is out of control if you do not:
>
> - Know exactly what your customers require
> - Have well-defined processes for translating those requirements into internal actions
> - Align all of your tasks and processes along common goals and objectives
> - Use key measures to manage by fact
> - Involve everyone in continuous improvement
> - Understand and improve all your critical processes
> - Satisfy your customers"[22]

The notion of viewing a business and its processes as a system seems intuitive if you accept the view that those processes have to work together as an integrated whole to achieve a common goal of maximizing customer value. However, very few businesses have really adopted systems thinking in the way they manage their business:

> "Most people are not used to thinking about their organizations in this way. We are dealing with complex structures here, from the operation of a company to the dynamics of a changing marketplace. People struggle to understand how it all fits together. They puzzle over where to begin. They lack the discipline for seeing wholes. 'Systems thinking is the antidote to feeling overwhelmed and helpless,' Senge writes. 'It offers a language that begins by restructuring how we think.'
>
> "The new management model accomplishes all this by focusing the entire company on the customer, then identifying and improving the processes that lead to customer satisfaction . . . The new model is directed toward results, which provide the link between customer requirements and the company's system."[23]

Adopting a systems thinking approach typically requires creating a mental model of the organization and its processes. The value of doing that is significant:

- It provides a simplified way of better understanding the cause-and-effect relationships that contribute to achieving business results.

- It serves as a common frame of reference that everyone in the organization can relate to and understand how their efforts contribute to the goals of the business as a whole.

- An understanding of how the processes currently work as a baseline point of reference is essential for effectively implementing ongoing improvement and reengineering initiatives.

Figure 3.1 shows an example of a simple high-level, conceptual diagram of how Cessna Aircraft views its organization from a systems perspective.

Systems thinking is *not* a new concept. It is based on systems theory that has evolved over the past 50 years as a way of modeling and understanding complex systems:

> "Systems theory or systems science argues that however complex or diverse the world that we experience, we will always find different types of organization in it, and such organization can be described by principles which are independent from the specific domain at which we are looking. Hence, if we would uncover those general laws, we would be able to analyze and solve problems in any domain, pertaining to any type of system. The systems approach distinguishes itself from the more traditional analytic approach by emphasizing the interactions and connectedness of the different components of a system."[24]

The idea of applying systems thinking to business systems gained significant attention with the original publication of Peter Senge's book *The Fifth Discipline* in 1990. Senge's ideas were very sound. Why then are people not applying them in actual practice on a more widespread basis? George and Weimerskirch express a possible explanation:

> "Responding to intense competition in a rapidly changing world, [managers] have been forced to seek other ways to be competitive. Many devour the closest meals first, laying people off, selling businesses, demanding more from those who remain. Eventually these sources run dry. At this point, leaders and managers turn their full attention to their companies, to the system they lead and

manage, and while many notice the 'hoof prints' of inefficiencies, errors, dissatisfaction, high costs, slow responses, and defecting customers, they cannot see the sources of these problems . . . They know their companies could do significantly better if they could only focus everybody's attention on what was important, but what is important? Where do we look first? How do we make sense of this complex, confusing system we call our company? How do we attack something we cannot see?"[25]

Managers have been looking for an easy way out, but as Senge points out, "the easy way out usually leads back in"[26] and there is obviously a limit to what can be gained without investing the time and effort to develop a more systemic approach:

". . . in reality, some companies simply downsize their existing organizations, call it reengineering, and force fewer people to do the same work they did before. While we understand that market realities will sometimes force businesses to take drastic steps, we question this approach. Companies who simply slash staff without re-thinking how they operate will sacrifice customer service at a time when the marketplace demands ever-higher service levels."[27]

Systems thinking is not something that only applies to the top-level managers, it needs to permeate the whole company at all levels to have maximum impact. Processes are implemented and managed by people on a day-to-day basis, the effectiveness of those people in many cases is one of the most important elements of overall process performance and it is often overlooked. Implementing a systems thinking approach requires tools that address:

- *Enterprise Modeling*—How do all the processes in the company fit together at a high level and how are they aligned with achieving the company's critical success factors?

- *Process Mapping*—At a process level, what are the activities, tasks, responsibilities, systems, and decisions in a process and how do they all fit together?

- *Lifecycle Models*—How does the company successfully manage efforts and changes that take place over a period of time and manage the risks associated with them? (Either high-level marketing and business strategy changes to adapt to market or technology changes or more tactical efforts such as product development projects.)

See Appendix B for references to available tools and resources.

As was previously mentioned, companies who use systems thinking generally have a different way of looking at things. They know and understand how their business operates from a systems perspective and they tend to understand management approaches, quality standards, and improvement methodologies at a deeper level. They understand the principles behind the approach and see how those principles might be used to help improve their business performance. They are able to assimilate multiple approaches easily into their business model because they see them only as tools, not as paradigms to completely redefine how their business is managed.

In some cases, it is not even obvious that the companies who use systems thinking have implemented some of these approaches, because they are so well assimilated into their business and they have adapted the approach as needed to fit with the way their business is managed. Table 3.2 shows a few examples.

Table 3.2   Examples of a systems-thinking approach.

Method	Typical Approach	Systems Approach
Six Sigma	Company adopts Six Sigma as a management paradigm and it completely redefines the way the company manages the business. The company sees itself as a Six Sigma company. Six Sigma may be overlaid over the existing organizational structure and organizations within the company are typically given quotas to achieve for Six Sigma cost reductions. It may not be well integrated with other related efforts within the company. It is very apparent that the company is doing Six Sigma because it defines the whole company and the implementation of Six Sigma typically follows a highly prescribed approach.	The company already has a well-established understanding of how its business operates from a systems perspective and has integrated Baldrige criteria and other best practices into a high-performance management system. This company sees Six Sigma not as an opportunity to redefine the way the business is managed, but just as a tool to help them become more effective. Their implementation of Six Sigma is typically more sophisticated. Instead of mechanically implementing a prescribed approach for Six Sigma, they take time to understand the principles behind it, adapt them to their business, and blend it in with other parts of the management system. It is less obvious that they are doing Six Sigma because it is so well assimilated into their business.

Continued

Table 3.2   Examples of a systems-thinking approach   *Continued*

Method	Typical Approach	Systems Approach
Balanced scorecard	Companies sometimes attempt to completely redefine their company around a Balanced Scorecard approach. The implementation of the Balanced Scorecard approach is very comprehensive, but may not adequately consider all of the other factors that need to be integrated with it to make the whole approach successful.	Systems-oriented companies see the Balanced Scorecard idea and the principles behind it as an excellent modeling tool to help them understand how their business system works from a metrics perspective and it provides a nice framework for developing a more hierarchical cause-and-effect relationship among the metrics that drive the business.

They see it only as a tool and only one tool among others that are needed for implementing a more effective business management system. |
| **ISO 9000** | Companies many times take a very superficial approach to implementing ISO 9000. They write procedures and work instructions that are designed from a compliance perspective to satisfy the auditors and add little value to the business. Their procedures exactly follow what is in the ISO standard and actually mimic what the standard says, word-for-word in some cases.

They hang the "ISO 9000 banner" on the side of the building to proclaim themselves as an ISO 9000 company. | More sophisticated companies take the time to interpret the principles and logic behind the requirements in the ISO standard and to more fully understand how it applies to their business. They start with a business model that is based around a systems approach for making their business operate effectively.

They do not mimic what is in the ISO standard; they simply use it as a checklist of best practices to validate the way they are managing the business. Any ISO requirements are fully integrated into their normal business management system with any other standards and management tools that may be relevant. |
| **Knowledge management** | Company attempts to redefine itself around knowledge management, to the extent of tracking the value of knowledge as a balance sheet item. It becomes a program that is implemented throughout the company on a widespread basis. | More sophisticated companies understand the value of knowledge management as an important tool to leverage their business. It is such a vital part of the way the business is run that it might not even be highly visible as "knowledge management." |

CREATION OF A LEARNING ORGANIZATION ENVIRONMENT

Systems thinking is only one component of the culture needed to create a learning organization. Rapidly assimilating information and acting on it to learn how to achieve higher levels of competitive customer value requires an environment where people thrive on continuous learning and improvement. The key characteristics that are essential to develop in this type of environment are:

- The organization and the people in it are open to looking at themselves honestly and objectively and recognizing opportunities for improvement.

- Everyone in the organization understands the overall vision and how their role contributes to that vision.

- There is an atmosphere that promotes learning throughout the organization and sharing of learning to maximize the knowledge embedded in the organization.

There is a maturity curve associated with developing effective and well-integrated quality and business management systems that typically looks something like Figure 3.2.

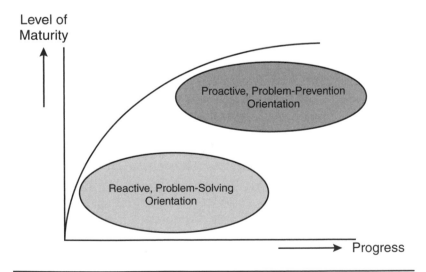

Figure 3.2 Level of Maturity learning curve.

Companies that are at a low level of maturity are typically characterized by a reactive, problem-solving orientation, as shown in Figure 3.2. This approach usually has a high level of firefighting associated with it. In fact, many companies are stuck in this mode and never get out of it. Some companies are so engrained in this mode of operation that it tends to shape their culture. In this type of company, the heroes are the firefighters that pull the customer out of the fire.

There is an old arcade game called "Whack-a-Mole" that illustrates this point well. In the arcade game, the player faces a game board full of holes and is armed with a rubber mallet. A "mole" pops up randomly in each of the different holes and the object of the game is to "whack" the "mole" every time it pops up. Of course, it just keeps popping up in different holes no matter how many times you hit it.

The approach to quality in this environment is very similar. Every time a problem comes up, there is an attempt to fix the problem, but it just keeps popping up over and over again in different places. The company never takes the time to get to the real root cause and to develop a proactive and systemic solution to prevent it from happening again.

This type of curve is called a *learning curve*; companies who learn from their mistakes and take action to prevent them from happening again move up the curve rapidly. Others, who simply stamp out problems as they occur, are stuck in the reactive corner and, many times, never move up the curve at all.

Winning the Race for Value very clearly describes what makes the difference in a learning organization:

> "The big difference between learning and nonlearning organizations is not measured in their capacity for error but in their capacity to respond to error. Persistence in error is a sure sign of an organization which, in today's politically correct parlance, is 'learning-challenged'. . . .
>
> "But don't be fooled. Dumb organizations are not necessarily staffed by dumb people. In fact, there may be many very smart people in a dumb organization. They are trapped there by a brain-dead organizational apparatus and are often very frustrated. The learning disability usually lies at the organizational level, not with the individual."[28]

The field of aviation is an excellent example of how these principles have been put into practice very effectively. Anytime there is a serious aircraft accident, there is a significant effort to discover the root cause of the accident and to take action, if necessary, to prevent it from happening again.

As a result, aviation safety has continued to improve dramatically over the years.

In today's complex world, learning is not as simple as it once was. The traditional approach has been to send people through massive amounts of training to cram them full of knowledge. That approach clearly has limitations. In many situations, it is impractical for people to learn beforehand all the facts and knowledge needed to do their jobs more effectively. Knowledge management systems, which will be discussed in chapter 7, can play an important role to supplement traditional learning approaches and significantly enhance the organization's ability to capture learning experiences and share it throughout the organization.

ENDNOTES

1. International Organization for Standardization, *ANSI/ISO/ASQ Q9004-2000 Quality management systems—Guidelines for performance improvements* (Geneva: International Organization for Standardization, 2000).
2. J. M. Kouzes and B. Z. Posner, *The Leadership Challenge* (San Francisco: Jossey-Bass, 1995): 15–16.
3. Ibid., 10–11.
4. J. Collins, *Good to Great* (New York: HarperCollins Publishers, 2001).
5. http://web66.coled.umn.edu/new/MLK/MLK.html.
6. "Sprint Quality Role Models," *The Point for all Sprint Employees* (March 2002): 5.
7. M. Hammer, *Beyond Reengineering* (New York: HarperCollins, 1996): 99.
8. Ibid., 100.
9. R. S. Kaplan and D. P. Norton, *The Balanced Scorecard* (Cambridge, MA: Harvard Business School Press, 1996): 24.
10. M. Treacy and F. Wiersena, *Discipline of Market Leaders* (Reading, MA: Addison-Wesley, 1995): 12.
11. Ibid.
12. Ibid.
13. Ibid.
14. See note 7.
15. See note 10.
16. T. H. Davenport, *Process Innovation* (Cambridge, MA: Harvard Business School Press, 1993): 160.
17. See note 7.
18. "Cessna aims to drive SCM to its very core," *Purchasing* (June 6, 2002): 31–35.
19. *The American Heritage Dictionary* (New York: Dell Publishing, 1983).
20. *Webster's Third New International Dictionary of the English Language* (Springfield, MA: Merriam Webster, 1986).

21. P. Senge, *The Fifth Discipline: The Art and Practice of the Learning Organization* (New York: Currency DoubleDay, 1990): 68–69.

22. S. George and A. Weimershirch, *Total Quality Management* (New York: John Wiley & Sons, 1994): 4–5.

23. Ibid., 5–9.

24. F. Heylighen, C. Joslyn, and V. Turchin, "Cybernetics and System Theory," http://pespmc1.vub.ac.be/CYBSWHAT.html.

25. See note 22: 1–3

26. See note 21: 60.

27. Business Architects, "Repositioning Reengineering," http://www.busarch.com/papers.

28. B. Sheehy, H. Bracey, and R. Frazier, *Winning the Race for Value* (American Management Association, 1996): 126.

4

Designing Integrated Management Systems

CHAPTER OVERVIEW

Implementing a strategy for business excellence requires developing a more integrated and cross-functional approach to management. To achieve that goal, it is essential to develop an understanding of how the business works as a system.

This chapter discusses modeling approaches that can be used to define how the business works as a system at several levels (enterprise model as well as detailed process maps and lifecycle models). These models essentially provide a "blue print" or "circuit schematic" of how the business works and help define a management system of how it is managed.

An integrated management system is one that integrates all requirements of the business (quality, business, and other requirements) into a single management system that is designed to maximize customer satisfaction and business results. Developing an integrated management system approach is becoming a necessity for effective systems that are designed for continuous improvement.

Figure 4.1 shows the general model that has been previously discussed for an integrated management system.

There is much to be learned from the software engineering discipline and the systems engineering approach associated with it for designing and developing complex systems. Applying a systems engineering approach to business systems yields benefits similar to the design of complex engineering systems:

• It is a multifaceted approach which considers all aspects of the design and is typically based on a collaborative team approach. The involvement of the major stakeholders in the process, as well as the key

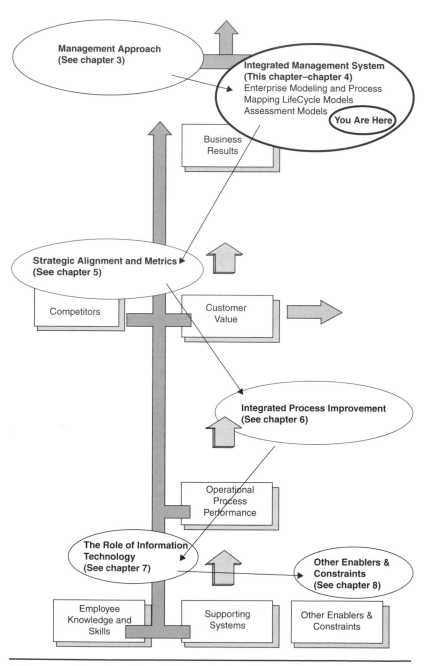

This navagational roadmap is intended to help readers understand the flow of information in these chapters and see how various topics fit into the overall model.

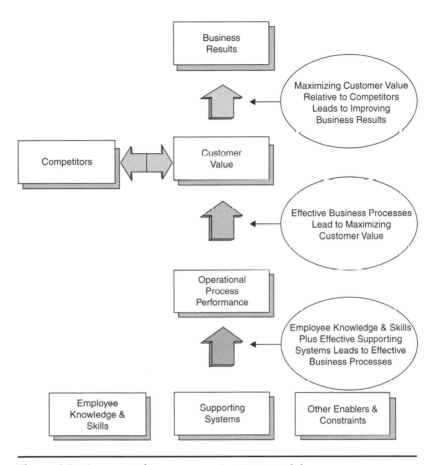

Figure 4.1 Integrated management system model.

contributors to the design effort as a team, will be more likely to result in a design approach that considers and meets all the requirements.

• It involves some discipline to ensure that all of the requirements for the design are clearly understood and documented before the design begins. Ensuring that the requirements are complete reduces the potential for redesign because some aspect of the design was not considered, and documenting the requirements reduces the potential for miscommunication and misunderstanding among all the participants in the design effort.

• It is a top-down, structured approach—the design is laid out at a block diagram level that identifies the major subsystems and interactions before a more detailed design effort takes place. The value in this approach is that it provides a mechanism to break down a very complex problem into more manageable components and preserves continuity with the top-level system design requirements.

In the design of complex software systems, a hierarchy of specifications at a system level, design level, and component level is sometimes developed to describe the interaction of what the system and its component parts must do to achieve a desired result. These items in the specifications are typically linked to items in test plans to validate that the system is actually doing what it was intended to do. In general, the same concept can be applied to business systems. For example:

- Define the requirements that the overall system must meet.

- Identify the critical subsystems (core processes), their roles in the overall model, and how they interact with each other.

- Further decompose the critical subsystems into lower levels of detail to understand how the elements are designed to achieve the objectives of that subsystem (process maps).

- Design instrumentation (metrics) to measure the effectiveness of the overall system and the subsystems.

- Develop a method to identify problems as they occur so that the system will be reliable and self-correcting (assessment and management review process).

Of course, the complexity of this effort in actual practice is going to depend on the nature of the business.

THE ROLE OF QUALITY STANDARDS AND BEST PRACTICES

The best approach for designing an integrated management system is to start with an enterprise model of how the business should ideally work to maximize effectiveness and then use any relevant standards and best practices as a checklist to validate that the management system is optimally designed to meet the requirements. An ideal management system should not attempt to mimic a particular standard or quality program; it should be designed to maximize the effectiveness of the business from a systems perspective in providing high levels of customer satisfaction and business results.

Quality standards should be used as a checklist of best practices to validate the design of the management system and *should not be used to define the design of the management system*. The problems that have been common in the implementation of quality and business management systems based on quality standards have typically resulted from:

1. Superficial implementations that attempt to mimic the requirements of the quality standard and do not take time to understand how it can be used as a tool to improve the business. This is typically associated with systems that are designed to satisfy the auditors and add little or no value to the business. In addition to reducing the effectiveness of the quality system, this approach creates a number of other problems:

- Typically, the quality manual and the design of the management system mimics exactly what the standard says. For example, in the implementation of the ISO standard, it was quite common to see policies and procedures that exactly followed the numbering of the ISO standard. When changes to the standard come out (such as the year 2000 version of ISO 9000), it may become necessary to almost totally redefine the quality system to map to the new numbering convention.

  A far better approach is to define the management system around the way the business actually works and simply cross-reference it to the elements of the ISO standard as necessary. If the standard changes, it is a simple matter of updating the cross-references rather than redefining the whole system.

- Integration of multiple standards can be a nightmare. Which standard do you mimic and how do you integrate the two sets of requirements? Using the cross-reference approach described above, it is only a matter of validating that the management system design meets the requirements of all appropriate standards and adding additional cross references as necessary.

- An approach that mimics a quality standard typically results in a management system that is defined in terms of quality requirements, not in terms of how the business actually operates, which provides very limited value as a management tool. Quality documents that are written for the benefit of the auditors to read also have limited value.

  On the other hand, if the process definitions are defined graphically in a way that makes them more understandable to the people performing the process, and are defined in a hierarchical way around the way the processes are actually managed, they become more of a useful tool that might actually be used by someone other than the auditors.

2. Implementing the quality standard as a quality program without making it an integral part of the business management system. This type of system usually regards "quality" as something that can be delegated to the quality department and fails to recognize its role in driving customer satisfaction and business results. There are several obvious problems with this approach:

- Organizational conflict and poor utilization of resources due to misalignment of goals within the company.

- Inadequate focus on customer satisfaction and quality due to limited visibility of its impact on the business.

- This type of organization is typically characterized by a reactive and corrective approach to quality. Often there is a relatively weak and poorly integrated framework for developing a more proactive and planned approach to maximize quality and customer satisfaction that is well aligned with business goals.

In order to avoid these problems, it is essential to provide broad-based training to the managers in the organization to help them understand the quality standards and how they apply to their organizations. They can then ensure that the design of their processes and their management system is consistent with any requirements and best practices that may be appropriate. One approach that works well is to combine a training session with a cross-functional self-assessment with the senior management team. Using this approach and the assessment tool described in Appendix B to capture and summarize the results:

- A facilitator goes through each item of the assessment model, which might be a quality standard or a customized assessment model specifically designed for the company's business with the senior management team.

- As the facilitator goes through the criteria, the senior management team is asked to discuss how that requirement affects their business, how important it is, how effectively they believe that they meet the requirement, and, finally, how difficult it is to make further improvement.

- At the end of the session the results of the assessment data can be sorted in different ways to answer a number of different questions, such as: Where are the items that have the weakest implementation that would have the least difficulty to address ("low-hanging fruit")? Or, Where are the items that are the most important to the business that have the weakest implementation?

A self-assessment like this can be a very effective approach for several reasons:

- It builds cross-functional consensus on the assessment results.

- It creates "buy-in" and understanding of the importance of the assessment criteria.

- As a result, there is likely to be a much higher level of support among the management team for taking action on the results.

Figure 4.2 shows how the ISO 9000 and Baldrige standards fit into this integrated management system model.

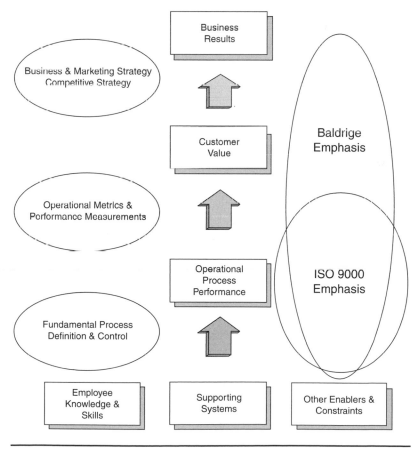

Figure 4.2   Relationship between quality standards.

There is some overlap in the coverage of the two standards as shown, but both potentially complement each other:

- Baldrige provides a very important linkage to driving business results that ISO doesn't provide.

- ISO provides a much stronger focus on operational process requirements, particularly those related to product and service quality.

- Six Sigma provides an excellent methodology for defining and implementing process improvement initiatives that goes beyond both ISO and Baldrige, but is another dimension on this chart that is not shown.

In most cases, limiting the design of the management system to a single standard will not yield optimal results; however, only a few companies have attempted to mix and match the requirements of the Baldrige criteria, the ISO 9000 standard and its industry variants, and a Six Sigma approach to process improvement. In some cases, they are perceived as competitive "programs." In fact, they can be very complementary and there is no reason why they cannot be used together. An ideal system could easily combine all of these requirements:

- The process management foundation and compliance requirements that ISO provides

- The additional linkages to business results and higher level functions, such as strategic planning and leadership, that Baldrige provides

- A disciplined approach to process improvement that Six Sigma provides

The following are some examples of companies who have successfully combined more than one of these approaches into an integrated management system:[1]

Ames Rubber Corporation:

"Baldrige gives Ames an overarching set of criteria questions to determine where we are, ISO helps us document what we're doing, and Six Sigma helps us to implement the processes to correct the problems. . . . each organization has to choose what best serves its needs."   —Tim Marvil, President and CEO

Eastman Chemical Company:

"Eastman has operated under the principles of the Baldrige Criteria as well as ISO 9000 for over 10 years . . . The company's quality management system is underpinned by the Baldrige principles, though expressed in a manner specific to the Eastman culture . . . ISO lays a foundation for necessary procedural standardization and we benefited most from ISO implementation in the creation of maintainable systems for process documentation and training. This helped us to significantly reduce variability. But, we have not used ISO as a means of instituting broader quality management, Eastman often had existing management processes that already met those requirements. The Baldrige principles were key to the development of many of these systems."

—Joe Wilson, Director of Corporate Quality

STMicroElectronics:

ST finds that even though ISO, Six Sigma, and the Baldrige Criteria for Performance Excellence may overlap in some areas, they are not mutually exclusive. "While each of these quality programs builds a foundation for continuous improvement, each is different in its scope and focus of its coverage . . .

"As we at ST see it, the Baldrige criteria lay the foundation for the entire organizational process by encouraging review of its approach . . .

"ISO addresses systems that have a direct influence in product quality and customer satisfaction, without suggesting tools for analysis, prioritization, and evaluation . . .

"Finally, Six Sigma addresses the statistical strategy philosophy for continuous improvement . . .

"Regardless of which tools suit the organization's needs, best-in-class companies continue to use them in their pursuit of performance excellence and their commitment to never be satisfied. In fact, all are mutually complementary and have their place in total quality management at ST."   —Richard Pieranunzi, President

The assessment tool discussed in Appendix B provides a capability to develop a customized assessment model, which might be a combination of criteria from several standards plus any other industry best practices that are appropriate.

ENTERPRISE MODELING AND PROCESS MAPPING

None of the approaches for designing integrated management systems or implementing effective process improvement initiatives can be done effectively without some way to define and visualize an overall enterprise model of how the organization works, as well as more detailed process maps describing how the processes are defined to support the goals of the enterprise model.

Enterprise Modeling

The role of enterprise modeling in this approach is extremely critical because it provides a visual representation of a system from a particular perspective and is essential to communicate complex relationships. The enterprise model is intended to define the higher-level view of how the major functions of the organization fit together in the "big picture." It is normally supported by more detailed process maps that define the detailed processes within each major functional area of the enterprise model. An example of an enterprise model of a business is shown in Figure 4.3. This is a very general model; a more specific and more detailed model is shown in the example at the end of this chapter. (See Figure 4.8 on page 78)

This model provides a high-level enterprise process view of the business and allows "drilling down" into further detail of the lower-level processes that make up each of these higher-level processes. It provides a way for business managers to easily understand the major components of a system as well as how they fit together and interact with each other from a business process perspective.

Figure 4.7 shows an example of an actual enterprise model that is very complete. Only the detailed numerical metrics have been excluded for confidentiality reasons. Some of the tasks that might normally be included in the development of an enterprise model would be:

- Develop purpose and mission statement to define the strategic vision for the organization.

- Define goals, business objectives, and short-term measurable results to be achieved.

Product Lifecycle   Operations Process

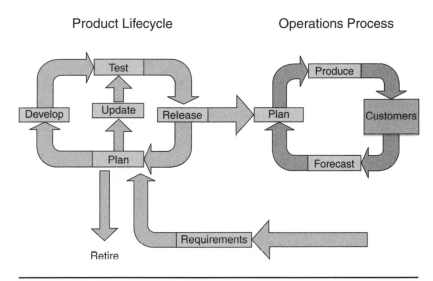

Figure 4.3   Enterprise model example.

- Identify shared beliefs and values that will be essential to shape the culture of the organization in achieving it's mission and objectives.

- Define the core processes and management structure that will be used to manage the organization.

The enterprise model serves several purposes:

- First, it helps the senior management team define how the organization works at a very high level and to define a management approach with goals and metrics to achieve the company's mission and objectives.

- Second, it is a tool to help all employees in the company see how everything fits together and to help them understand how their own roles fit into the "big picture."

Process Mapping

The ANSI/ISO/ASQ 9000-2000 standard says "The organization shall:

a. Identify the processes needed for the quality management system and their application throughout the organization

b. Determine the sequence and interaction of these processes

c. Determine criteria and methods to ensure that both the operation and control of these processes are effective

d. Ensure the availability of resources and information necessary to support the operation and monitoring of these processes

e. Monitor, measure, and analyze these processes

f. Implement actions necessary to achieve planned results and continual improvement of these processes"[2]

It does not explicitly require graphical process maps, but one could very easily infer that a textual description of how a process works is going to be very limited, in many cases, as a tool to fully understand a company's business processes.

A variety of tools are available today to provide a capability for mapping the details of process flows. Many of these tools also provide a capability for hierarchical organization of processes as well as a capability for simulating the actual operation of a process for cycle time analysis and activity-based costing types of analysis.

Figure 4.4 shows an example of a high-level process map and Figure 4.5 shows a more detailed view of one of the processes. Many of the activities in these maps drill down into progressively lower levels of detail. (Figure 4.5 is a drill-down of Process Block 11 "Order Review and Acceptance Process" in the higher-level example map.) The process map can be combined and linked with any relevant documents and can be annotated with notes related to specific tasks in the process. This type of process presentation is much more effective than some of the textual procedure and work instruction descriptions that have been used in the past for several reasons:

• The graphics allow visualizing the flow of the process and the interrelationship of the activities that comprise the process.

• By providing a drill-down capability, the presentation of the process information is simplified. Rather than overwhelming people with an infinite amount of process detail, a simplified high-level view of the process can be combined with more detail at a lower level if it is needed. That allows the information in the maps to be used by a variety of people with different levels of interest in the process. For example, managers may only be interested in a high-level view of how the process works, while someone who is responsible for performing some portion of the process may be more interested in the detail.

Many typical ISO 9000 procedures and work instructions as they were designed in the past were primarily for the benefit of the auditors. They provided a way for companies to prove to the auditors that they had a well-defined and documented way of performing a process. In truth, however, many were not completely effective in providing a tool that helped people more effectively perform the process. A graphical process map not only satisfies the ISO 9000 requirement to have well-defined and documented processes, but it is also generally more effective as a tool to help people at various levels understand how the process works, its interrelationships, and the role they play in performing the process. It is also much more consistent with ISO 9000:2000 in promoting the idea of system thinking and understanding how all the processes and activities contribute to overall effectiveness.

AN EXAMPLE—DAIMLER-CHRYSLER FINANCIAL SERVICES ASIA/PACIFIC

My friend and colleague, Bill Bishop, has developed a very nice approach that put many of these ideas into actual practice with Daimler-Chrysler Financial Services Asia/Pacific and integrated the ISO 9000:2000 requirements into a very large international TQM project that is being completed in 2002. Figure 4.6 shows the major elements of the project.

The design of a business system should begin with a starting point, as shown in Figure 4.6 that defines the results the business management system is intended to achieve and the strategies and goals needed to accomplish those results. Bill acted as a facilitator with the senior management staff of Daimler-Chrysler Financial Services Asia/Pacific and helped them develop an overall enterprise model of the business organization, as shown in Figure 4.7. The senior management team integrated the enterprise model with:

- A statement of Purpose and Mission of the organization
- Shared Beliefs and Values
- Goals
- Core Processes
- Business Objectives, Critical Measures, and 2002 Targets

This document neatly summarizes a lot of information and became a unifying framework for integrating all aspects of the management system.

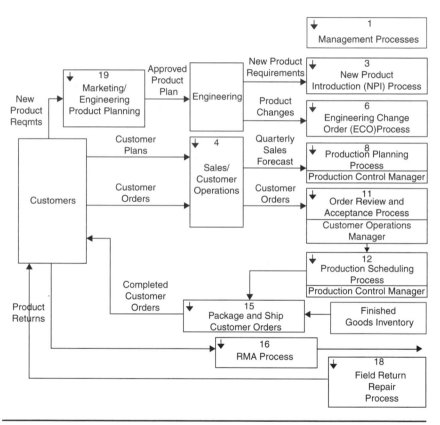

Figure 4.4   Example high-level process map.   *Continued*

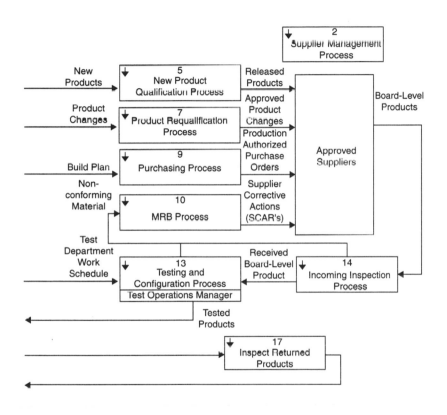

Figure 4.4 Continued.

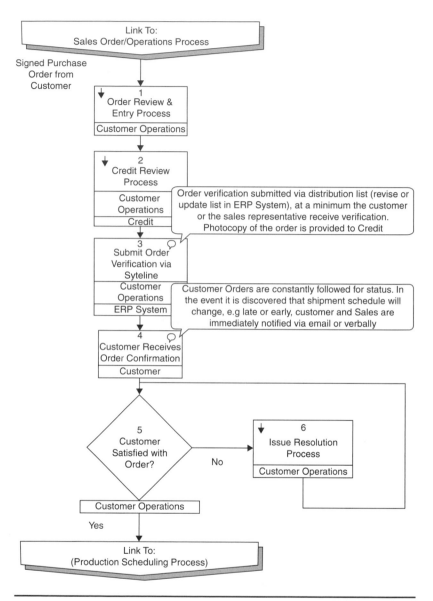

Figure 4.5 Example detail-level process map.

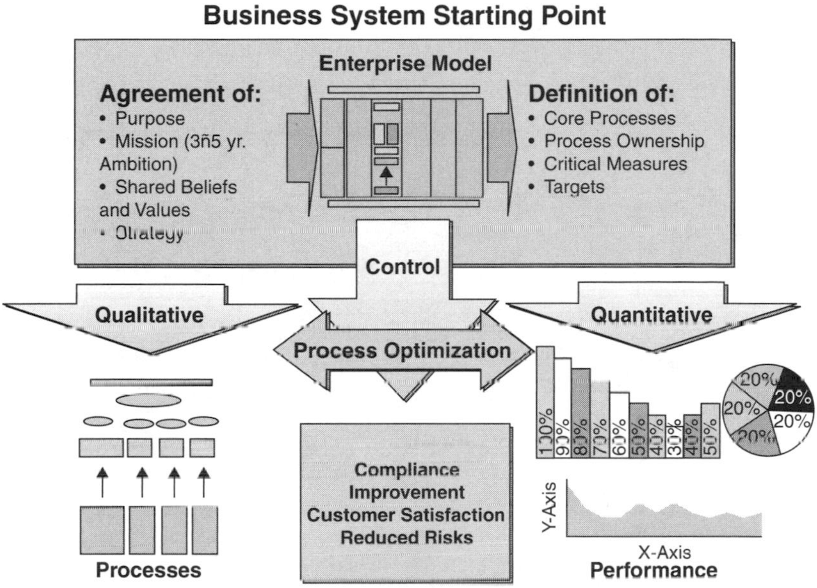

Business System Starting Point

Figure 4.6   Daimler-Chrysler Financial Services Project.

In addition to the high-level enterprise model shown in Figure 4.7, lower-level models were created for the major areas of business within the company, as shown in Figure 4.8 below:

At a corporate level, the business processes within the enterprise model were further broken down as follows:

1. *Governing Processes* define the fundamental management and administrative requirements that pertain to the business.

2. *Core Processes* document the operational activities within the core business processes:

   - Customer Support/Business Connect

   - Credit Risk Management

   - Passenger Car Business Development

   - Commercial Vehicle Business Development

   - Insurance Services

   - Fleet Services

Daimler-Chrysler

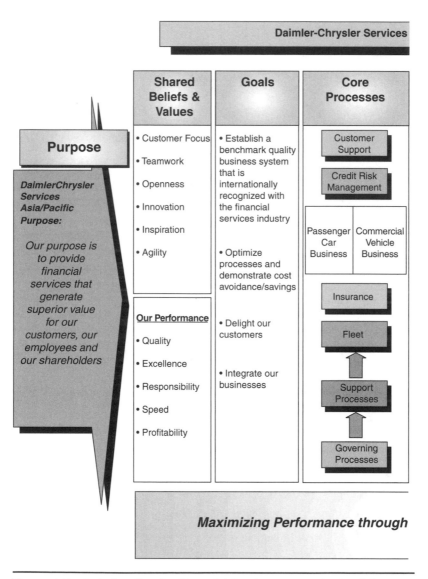

Figure 4.7 Daimler-Chrysler Financial Services Enterprise Model.

Continued

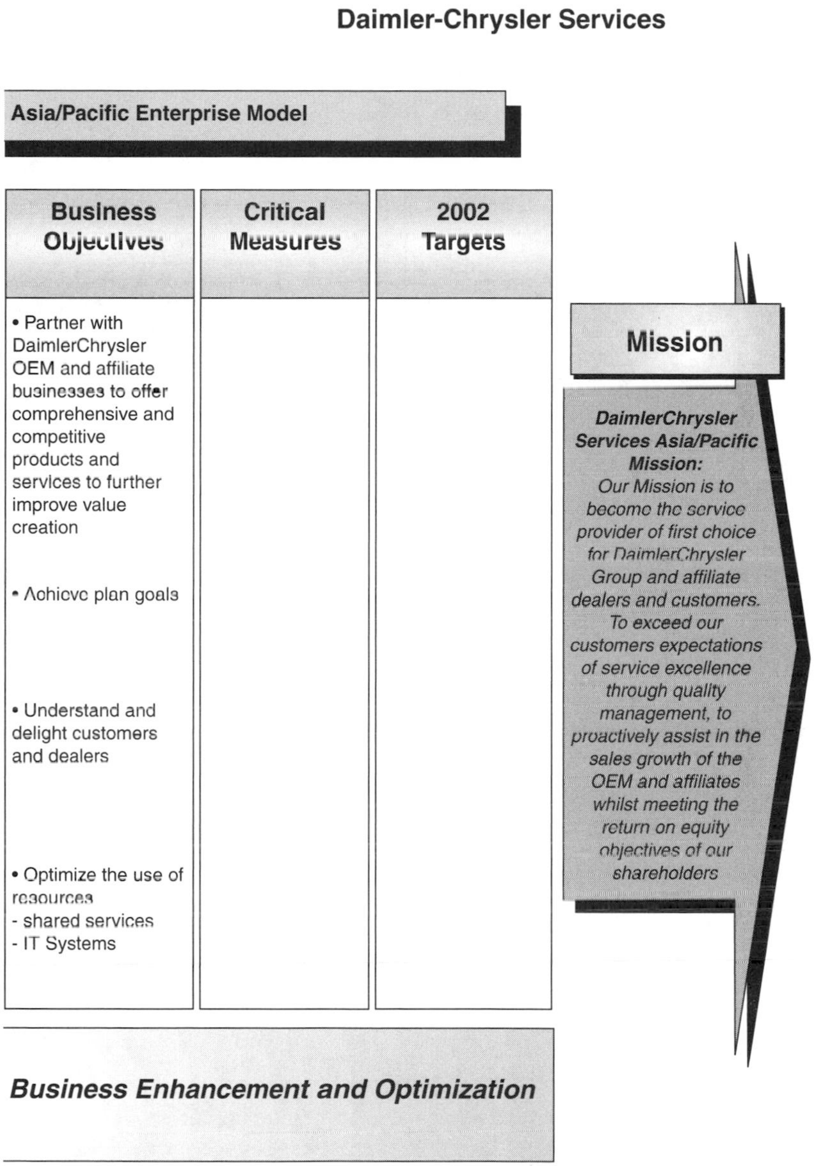

Daimler-Chrysler Services

Asia/Pacific Enterprise Model

Business Objectives	Critical Measures	2002 Targets
• Partner with DaimlerChrysler OEM and affiliate businesses to offer comprehensive and competitive products and services to further improve value creation		
• Achieve plan goals		
• Understand and delight customers and dealers		
• Optimize the use of resources - shared services - IT Systems		

Mission

DaimlerChrysler Services Asia/Pacific Mission:
Our Mission is to become the service provider of first choice for DaimlerChrysler Group and affiliate dealers and customers. To exceed our customers expectations of service excellence through quality management, to proactively assist in the sales growth of the OEM and affiliates whilst meeting the return on equity objectives of our shareholders

Business Enhancement and Optimization

Figure 4.7   Continued.

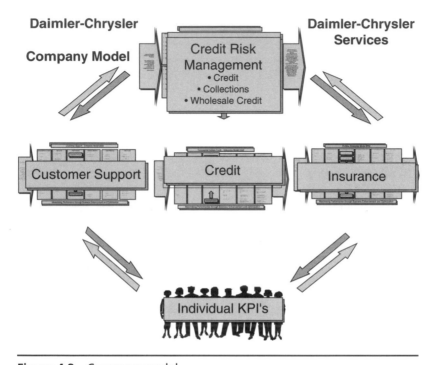

Figure 4.8   Company model.

3. *Support Processes* provide secondary inputs into the Core Processes. The effectiveness of the Core Processes is dependent on the effectiveness of the processes that support them:

   • Controlling and Planning

   • Corporate Business Services

   • IT Services

   • Legal Services

   • Human Resources

The governing processes, core processes, and support processes were then further defined into processes and subprocesses, as shown in Figures 4.9 through Figure 4.11.

The management system was then implemented at an individual country level at each of the following countries in the Asia/Pacific region:

   • Australia

   • Taiwan

- Japan

- Singapore

- Thailand

Having a well-defined model to define this implementation significantly streamlined the implementation of a new management system and resulted in a seamless integration throughout the Asia/Pacific region. Some of the benefits that came out of this project were that it:

• *Allowed the participants to gain an appreciation of the business in terms of its strategy, processes, objectives, measures, and targets.* Creation of the enterprise models had a unifying effect of helping everyone in the organization understand the operation of the business as a system.

• *Allowed the participants to gain an appreciation of the importance of defining the sequence and interaction of the business processes.* Clearly

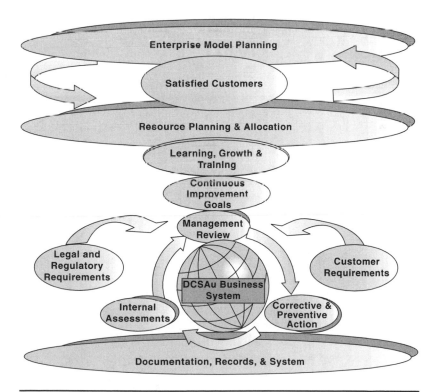

Figure 4.9   Daimler-Chrysler Services Australia governing processes.

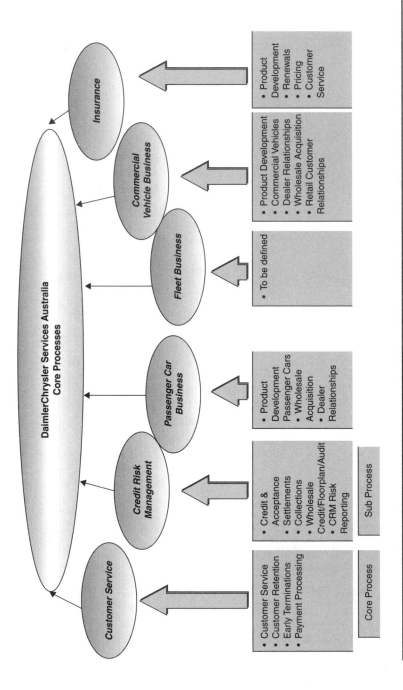

Figure 4.10 Daimler-Chrysler Services Australia core processes.

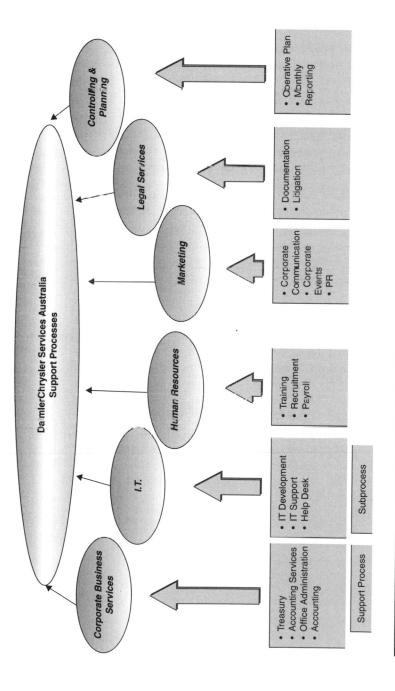

Figure 4.11 Daimler-Chrysler Services Australia support processes.

defining processes and decision points within the processes helped managers focus on determining how to more effectively manage risks in the business.

- *Demonstrated the flexibility of the enterprise model approach by customizing the model to the unique business needs of individual geographies.* Although many aspects of the model were standardized, the exact implementation of the processes in each geographic area was customized as needed to fit local requirements.

- *Demonstrated the value of a clear, process-based approach to business.* Implementation of the project included an extensive amount of employee and management involvement at all levels and resulted in some very positive changes in culture throughout the organizations in the Asia/Pacific region of Daimler-Chrysler Financial Services. For example, the models helped managers to see the business from more of a systems perspective and to better understand the interrelationships within the business. Having a common understanding of how the business functions as a system also led to higher levels of synergy and cross-functional collaboration among all areas.

As a follow-up effort, the same methodology was used to plan and define the implementation of a new startup business in Korea, and the use of this approach for planning and defining the business had a significant impact on accelerating the startup of that new business venture.

LIFECYCLE MODELS

The modeling approaches that have been discussed so far in this chapter are based on a snapshot in time of how the organization looks and how it's processes works. It is obvious, however, that there is also a time element that must be modeled:

- The businesses and markets that organizations are in change over time.

- As a result, product strategies change.

- In any dynamic organization, new product development efforts are constantly being initiated and each of these might also precipitate some process changes.

If business strategies, products, and processes were truly static, there would be less challenge to managing them, but in today's world that is rarely consistent with reality. In fact, probably the biggest risk to quality in any organization is successfully managing events that happen over a period of time and involve some kind of change in a business strategy, product, or process.

Lifecycle models provide a very important planning and integration framework for modeling and understanding this type of event that takes place over a period of time. The TL 9000 quality standard in the telecommunications industry has recognized the importance of lifecycle models and has made it a mandatory requirement for companies who are TL 9000 certified to document a lifecycle model defining how their business is managed.

Lifecycle models might be used to manage changes that may be very slow and gradual or very quick and dramatic. They might also be implemented at a number of different levels. A lifecycle model provides a number of benefits, including:

- Risk management

- Cross-functional integration

- Resource management

- Repeatability

- Continuous improvement

The following are some examples of different levels of lifecycle models.

Technology Lifecycles

As an example, Motorola is a technology innovator; they succeed by successfully developing and implementing new technology before anyone else in the market. They lose some of their advantage in the market when a technology reaches maturity and the primary success factor becomes producing a commodity product at the lowest possible cost. At that point, Motorola might make a decision to either continue or discontinue in that technology area. (Motorola actually made color television sets at one time, but got out of that market after it became a commodity product.)

Each technology has a lifecycle associated with it and this is naturally a very important part of Motorola's planning process. Figure 4.12 is a very simplified diagram to illustrate this (naturally, real life technology life cycle models can be much more complex than this simple illustration).

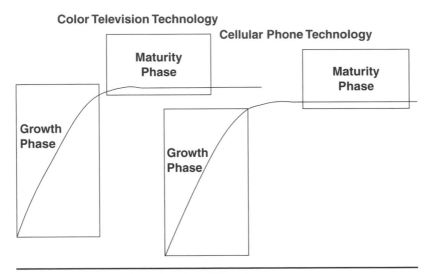

Figure 4.12   Example technology lifecycle.

It is obviously critical to Motorola's success to understand where they are in a given technology lifecycle. An incorrect decision at each decision point in the lifecycle model might cause the company to waste a significant amount of money and resources. Early in the lifecycle of a particular technology, it would probably be very appropriate to invest heavily in product development and seize a leading market share position in the market. Later in the lifecycle, as the technology approaches maturity, there would probably be much more limited benefit from further developing the technology with new products or features. A wise strategy at that point might be to minimize further investment in that technology area and move on to another area that is in the growth stage and offers higher returns.

A lifecycle model that is designed to manage this kind of change might consist of periodically reviewing the state of the market and the technology and making investment decisions appropriate to where it is in relation to the overall lifecycle. This is an example of a change that happens gradually over a period of time, and semi-annual or annual reviews might be sufficient for making this level of decision.

An evaluation of the completeness and effectiveness of a lifecycle model should be based on the risks that are being managed and their impact. A lifecycle model normally includes some review points where decisions are made. A good question to ask at each of these points in the lifecycle model is, "What is the impact of making a wrong decision, and is the frequency and completeness of decision points appropriate to mitigate the potential impact of those risks?" For example, the risks in this case are:

- Staying in a technology area too long and wasting money and resources on investing in product development in that area that might be better spent in another area

- Missing an opportunity to enter a new technology area or entering the market too late to gain sufficient market share to be successful

Product/Project Lifecycles

A decision to enter a new technology area (like cellular phones) would logically spawn some product development initiatives and development projects with that decision. Each of these products and projects would have a lifecycle associated with it, but product lifecycles are naturally very different from, but related to, technology lifecycles. Figure 4.13 shows how the different levels of lifecycle models might be interrelated.

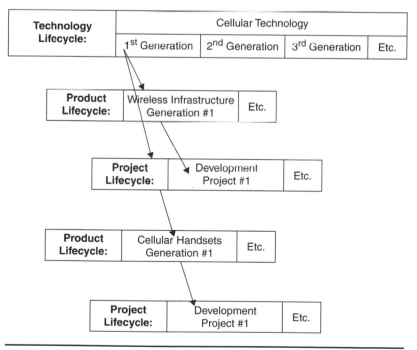

Figure 4.13 Interrelationship of lifecycle models.

A product lifecycle model might cover either a particular product, generation of product, or family of products. A project lifecycle model is one project within a product lifecycle model. For example, the Motorola "Star-TAC" was an early Motorola cellular handset product family that consisted of several models with different variations. A product lifecycle model would be used to manage that product or product family until it reaches end-of-life and is replaced by a next generation product.

That product lifecycle might spawn a number of different development projects. For example, there might be a development project lifecycle for each variation or revision of that particular "StarTAC" phone within the overall product lifecycle. There might also be project development lifecycles at different levels, such as the development of a new battery technology that might be needed to implement the phone. In the simplest case, a product lifecycle might be combined with a project lifecycle.

If there is a distinction between a product lifecycle and a project lifecycle, the product lifecycle might focus on the higher-level issues such as market release of the new product, sales readiness, and the need for testing customer response, while the project lifecycle would typically focus on the development requirements needed to support the higher-level strategy.

Figure 4.14 shows a simplified example of what a product/project development lifecycle might look like.

A lifecycle model that is designed for managing product and project lifecycles would typically consist of phases as shown, although some of the

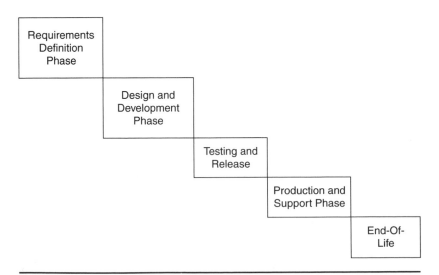

Figure 4.14   Example project development lifecycle.

effort might not be completely sequential as shown in the figure. A very critical task is to select or design a lifecycle model that is appropriate to the risks being managed. In general, there is a trade-off between tight risk management and time-to-market. For example, the "waterfall" model is a classic lifecycle model that has phases that are totally sequential, as shown in Figure 4.15, where one phase does not start until the requirements of the previous phase have been completed. This may result in improving control of risks, but might seriously extend time-to-market.

In the case of supply chains, where one company might provide products to another systems integrator (who has their own lifecycle model), there are typically very large opportunities for cycle time reduction by collaborating within the supply chain and overlapping some of the cycles in the lifecycles with a minimum of added risk. As an example, I worked with a software engineering manager at one time who told me, "My customers (system integrators) want products that have bugs in them. They know if they get totally bug-free products, they are getting them late in the development cycle and missing an opportunity for a considerable amount of cycle time improvement in their own lifecycle model."

That might horrify some people who are used to the traditional "quality control" approach that focuses primarily on control of defects. However, it makes perfect sense if you take the view that "quality" is much broader than reduction of defects; it also includes cycle time and any other variable that affects customer satisfaction and business results. Clearly, in this case, if there is a mutual understanding between the two companies regarding the risks of giving them an early release of a software product that might have bugs in it to improve cycle time, it could be a very reasonable thing to do. (The "bugs" will be corrected later before the systems integrator releases their product, but it provides a head start on the integration effort.)

A lifecycle model also does not have to be rigid; it is only a tool and isn't a substitute for good project management and sound decision making. For example, if at the completion of the testing and release phase, some portion of the testing requirements are incomplete, a risk management decision would normally be made. A reasonable decision might be made to go ahead and order some of the long lead-time parts required for the production and support phase based on an evaluation of the potential risks associated with the incomplete test requirements. The important point, however, is that *it is a conscious and well-thought-out decision* in light of the potential risks. (There is a big difference between that and someone just making a decision to go ahead without any understanding of the risks.) The lifecycle model provides a framework for making those decisions intelligently and obtaining whatever cross-functional buy-in may be needed to make the decision.

The Value of a Lifecycle Model

A lifecycle model serves several important purposes.

1. Risk Management

   There is naturally a risk associated with successfully completing any of these efforts being managed, and one of the key purposes of a lifecycle model is to serve as a risk management tool. A lifecycle model typically is broken into some number of phases depending on the risks and complexity of the effort being managed. Each phase typically has some completion criteria to evaluate the degree of completeness of the activities required by that phase. The purpose is to prevent errors that happen early in a lifecycle from propagating all the way through the remainder of the lifecycle. If an error or anomaly can be detected early, its impact is typically much lower, as shown in Figure 4.15.

   In this example, if a problem shows up in the design phase and is detected and corrected in the design phase, the impact is mini-

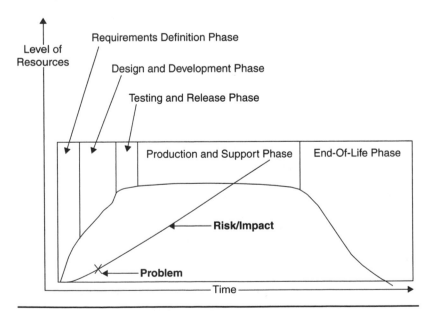

Figure 4.15 Lifecycle risk management.

mized. On the other hand, if the problem is not detected in the design phase and the product continues into testing and production, the impact could be much more substantial. Significant rework might be required or, in the worst case, some portion of the previous phases might need to be repeated to make sure the design is still consistent with its original requirements.

2. Cross-Functional Integration

A lifecycle model is an excellent tool for cross-functional integration because it provides a roadmap so that people understand how their role fits into the overall lifecycle in relationship to the other activities of other team members.

3. Resource Management

By providing a roadmap for engaging resources from different functions, resource management is also improved:

• Each functional organization can optimize the use of their resources by not engaging earlier than they are needed in the lifecycle model, and focusing their efforts on well-defined roles and tasks helps utilize the resources more effectively.

• Having completion requirements for each phase prevents false starts of engaging resources before the product is ready for them. (For example, releasing a product to manufacturing before it's ready would cause wasted resources.)

4. Repeatability

Another big advantage of a lifecycle model is repeatability. There is probably a much higher chance of success in using a proven methodology that has worked on previous projects of a similar nature than no methodology at all, a new unproven methodology that is created on the fly for the project, or one that doesn't really fit this kind of project.

5. Continuous Improvement

A lifecycle model serves as a baseline to define how to successfully manage an effort. A good practice in any lifecycle model is to do a post mortem at the end of the project to see how things went and what can be improved in the lifecycle model to improve the next time around. If that is done correctly, the lifecycle model gets better and better as time goes on. If there is no lifecycle model to use as a baseline and each project starts from scratch to define whatever methodology might seem appropriate, there is no basis for ongoing improvement.

Implementation Strategies

Lifecycle models are probably one of the most critical and highest impact areas in the design of an integrated business and quality management system, and it requires careful thought and planning. Some questions that might arise include:

1. How many different levels of lifecycles are needed?

   It depends on the nature of the business and the risks involved. If, for example, the business is stable and the technology is not changing significantly, it may not be necessary to have a high-level business or technology lifecycle, or its impact may be minimized.

2. How many different kinds of lifecycles are needed?

   At a project level, that primarily depends on how homogeneous the projects are. Trying to force-fit a lifecycle model onto a project that it is not appropriate for can have very negative effects, including wasting resources, increasing cycle time and costs unnecessarily, and increasing the risks in a project. In an organization I worked with at one time, we had three different lifecycle models that we used for development.

   • One was a "waterfall" model that is more appropriate for "start from scratch" design efforts with high risk.

   • Another was a "prototype" model that was appropriate for projects where it was difficult to conceptualize the requirements without building an initial prototype, and cycle time was significantly improved by abbreviating the full requirements definition process that would normally take place.

   • Another model was a "continuous development" model, which was designed for a product that was relatively stable but continued to evolve through incremental periodic enhancements.

3. How much customization and/or deviation from the lifecycle model should be allowed?

   It depends on the risks and the maturity of the project teams. Any lifecycle model is only a tool and cannot substitute for good project management discipline and skill. In an organization I worked with, we created a "Project Quality Plan" at the beginning of a project based on a template of normal lifecycle model requirements. The project team customized the Project Quality Plan as needed to fit the risks and complexity of the particular project and it was approved by the development manager. As long as the potential impact of the deviations is well understood and any potential impact on the project is acceptable, that is a perfectly reasonable approach. The same is true of deviations from phase transition requirements during the course of a project.

Many people have the perception that there is no room for judgment in an ISO 9000 quality system and it must be implemented rigidly; that is not the case and attempting to rigidly enforce some of these requirements where they've added little value is one thing that has given ISO 9000 and other quality systems a bad reputation. There is plenty of room for good judgment and intelligence in the implementation of these requirements in modern quality systems; however, the rules of how much deviation is acceptable and who has authorization to approve deviations and customization of the lifecycle model requirements should be defined.

Appendix A contains an example lifecycle model that can be used for business process improvement projects that contain a significant information systems component. A key objective of this lifecycle model is to ensure that the business requirements are well integrated with the design and implementation of the improvement initiative, including the associated information systems.

ENDNOTES

1. Baldrige National Quality Program, "Baldrige, Six Sigma, & ISO: Understanding Your Options," *CEO Issue Sheet* (summer 2002).
2. International Organization for Standardization, *ANSI/ISO/ASQ Q9000-2000 Quality management systems—Fundamentals and vocabulary* (Geneva: International Organization for Standardization, 2000).

5

Strategic Planning, Alignment, and Metrics

CHAPTER OVERVIEW

A business cannot operate as a system without a direction and purpose. A strategic plan is what provides the direction and creates a sense of purpose for everyone in the organization. Metrics are essential to evaluate the effectiveness of the strategic plan, determine whether the organization is making adequate progress against its goals, and integrate the organization around a consistent set of goals.

This chapter discusses how to use a strategic planning process and metrics as a unifying force to further integrate and align all aspects of the business around achieving its mission and goals.

THE ROLE OF A STRATEGIC PLAN

The importance of having a clear strategy and vision for an organization to provide a context for ongoing management of processes as well as developing and managing process improvement initiatives cannot be overemphasized:

> "Creating a strong and sustained linkage between strategy and the way work is done is an enduring challenge in complex organizations. Because business processes define how work is done, we are dealing with the relationship between strategy and process. Process innovation is meaningful only if it improves a business in ways that are consistent with its strategy. In fact, process innovation is impossible—or at least only accidental—unless the lens of process analysis is focused on a particularly strategic part of the business, with particular strategic objectives in mind . . .

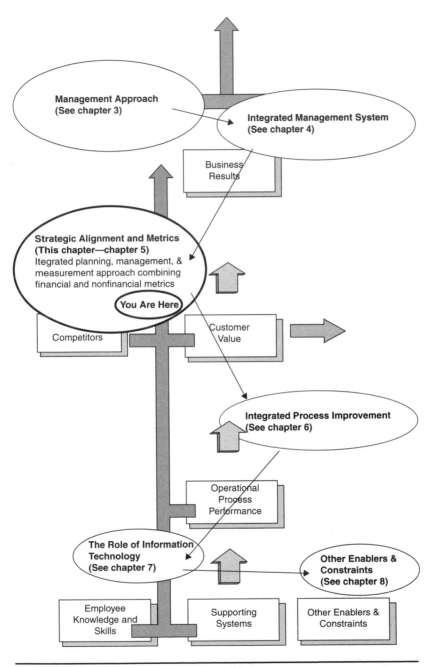

This navigational roadmap is intended to help readers understand the flow of information in these chapters and see how various topics fit into the overall model.

"Congruence or alignment between strategies and processes is essential to radical change in business processes. Strategy and process objectives must reinforce one another and echo similar themes ... Process change without strategy and vision seldom goes beyond streamlining, with a resulting incremental reduction in time and cost."[1]

There are actually two challenges here: one is the higher-level task of defining a strategic plan and redefining it as needed based on change; and the second is that once the plan is defined, using that vision as a unifying force to align and integrate all the efforts in the company around achieving that vision. It is outside the scope of this book to get too far into how to develop a strategic plan or what it should consist of; the primary focus here is on the role it plays in unifying and integrating the tactical execution to achieve success.

Strategic Vision

The research in *Good to Great* defines what it calls the "hedgehog" concept based on an essay by Isaiah Berlin.[2] In the story, the hedgehog is a slow and awkward creature that looks like a "genetic mix-up between a porcupine and a small armadillo." The hedgehog wins over-and-over again against a more cunning fox that is much more crafty and fleet of foot. Every time the fox attacks, the hedgehog simply rolls up into a perfect little ball with sharp spikes pointing outward in all directions.[3]

Good to Great identifies having a "hedgehog" concept that is a defining vision of:[4]

- What the company is deeply passionate about

- What the company can be the best in the world at

- What drives the company's economic engine

Having a "hedgehog" concept and sticking to it is one of the characteristics that distinguished a "great" company that has sustained "great" performance for at least 15 years in the research that was done by Jim Collins and his team.

It's important to recognize that having a strategic vision that is simple and unifies the company doesn't necessarily imply that the company is fixed and rigid in the way it does things. The following is an example of a strategic vision statement from Sprint:

"To be a world-class telecommunications company—the standard by which others are measured."

"A company's vision statement is the most fundamental expression of how it will grow profitable market share. Our vision is supported by the mission statements of each of our business units and corporate departments. Achieving our vision will rely on the successful pursuit of our goals and values.

"Our desire to be 'the standard by which others are measured' implies that we will continually redefine our industry by setting new standards for a telecommunications company's image, products and services, and business practices . . . something we have been doing for years."[5]

Strategic Alignment

One of the primary reasons both TQM and reengineering efforts in the 1990s failed to produce expected results in many cases was a lack of alignment with the company's overall strategic goals:

"Increasingly, questions are being asked about how effective restructuring and reengineering have been. In too many cases, the answers are mixed, profits do not improve, productivity remains low, and shareholder value does not increase. It is now becoming clear that many of the reengineering efforts of the early 1990s were mismanaged. Lacking any clear link to corporate strategy (sometimes reengineering was the strategy), these efforts became little more than brutal exercises in cutting costs."[6]

The quality movement has also recognized the need to link the historical views of quality control and quality assurance into the broader aspects of customer satisfaction and business results. In that context, quality means not only doing things right, but *doing the right things right* (for example, things that enhance customer value and satisfaction and lead to improved business results). This trend is clearly reflected in the Malcolm Baldrige National Quality Award criteria, which over the past few years has increasingly included more focus on business results.

As an example, Cadillac Motors won the Baldrige Award in 1990. Cadillac won the award at that time because they had substantially improved their product quality. The cars that they were producing at that point in time were of a much higher quality; however, Cadillac had not realigned the style and design of the cars they were building with customer values to be more competitive with other luxury car manufacturers.

This is a good example of how improving product quality does not necessarily lead to business success unless the improvements in quality are aligned with customer values. If Cadillac Motors in 1990 were reevaluated against the current Baldrige Award criteria, they probably would not have won the award, because the new criteria include much more emphasis on business results.

In many cases, there is a deeper cause behind these situations: either corporate strategic plans or goals were not well defined to begin with, and/or they became misaligned with the market over the course of the effort. In both of those cases, the weakness can be traced even further back to planning systems that were inadequate to clearly define goals and requirements and/or keep pace with changes in the market.

The strategic planning process in most companies is inadequate to provide sufficient direction to these efforts and to keep pace with changes in the marketplace. Many companies perform strategic planning once a year at best, and it may or may not be based on a formalized process for gathering the information needed to make the decisions required. In some cases, the information may be available but is not used effectively.

The ideal model is a management system that is tightly coupled with customer needs and expectations as well as competitive information, and has built-in mechanisms to continuously identify and implement areas for improvement and change, as shown in Figure 5.1. Probably the most important thing in this model is the input data that is used to drive the strategic planning process. *Winning the Race for Value* uses an analogy to a military general defending the city of Moscow from Tolstoy's *War and Peace* to illustrate this point very clearly:

> "Tolstoy introduces us to the general as he prepares to confront the French army. He is flooded with mutually exclusive recommendations from his staff. At the same time, he cannot pinpoint the exact location of the French army and possesses only fragmentary information about the locations and movements of his own divisions. When he calls for more information, what he receives is confusing and contradictory, forcing him to use intuition to separate rumor from fact."[7]

It is interesting to contrast that scenario with our more recent experience in the Persian Gulf War and the war in Afghanistan, where the integration of information technology and battlefield planning was far more advanced and had a very decisive impact on the outcome.

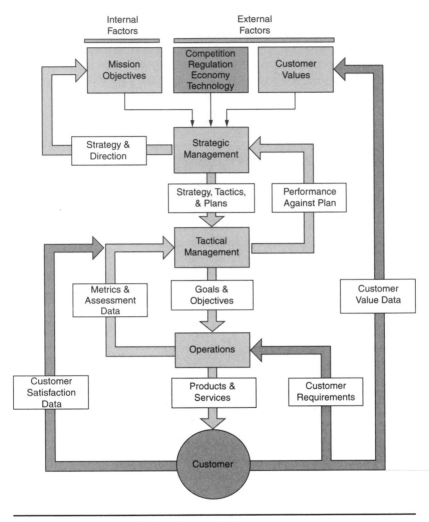

Figure 5.1   Integrated planning model.

There are a multitude of opportunities in any company for ongoing process improvement as well as more radical change. The strategic planning process provides the context for integrating those efforts with the company's business strategy. Companies can consume huge amounts of dollars and resources on these efforts, and unless those efforts are focused, prioritized, and carefully managed, the overall business results may not be predictable and will be unlikely to yield the maximum contribution.

In many companies, the linkages among these areas are very disjointed and they do not even speak the same language:

- Customers think in terms of quality and value.

- Business planning is focused on business results (generally financials).

- Operational management is focused on detailed process metrics.

To close this loop, we first need to adopt a common language: customer value is the mechanism that translates operational process improvements into business results, as shown in Figure 5.2.

To be able to use this model, it is necessary to answer the following questions:

- What is the relationship of customer value to business results? What customer behavior is most important to influence? What are the most critical motivators that influence that behavior?

- How will improvements in operational process performance impact value as perceived by the customer? What is the relationship to perceptions of competitors?

- What is the role of employee knowledge and skills and other constraints and enablers in overall process performance?

None of these questions can be answered precisely and the relationships are difficult to quantify; however, some assumptions can be made, a model can be built based on those assumptions, and the model can be continually refined based on actual experience.

THE BALANCED SCORECARD APPROACH

The Balanced Scorecard approach is based on exactly these ideas.[8] It generally consists of a hierarchy of metrics corresponding to the four levels shown in Figure 5.2 and provides a closed-loop methodology for integrating those metrics into the strategic planning and management cycle of the company. It translates an organization's mission and strategy into a comprehensive set of performance measures and provides the framework for a

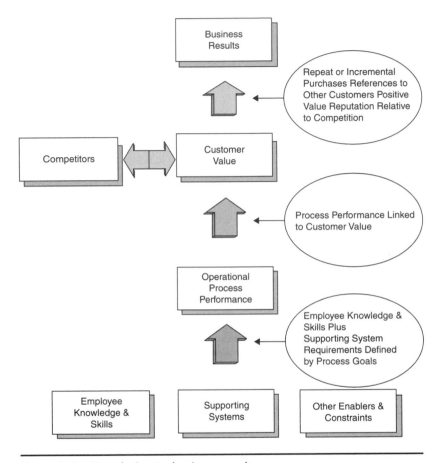

Figure 5.2 Translation to business results.

strategic measurement and management system. It is an excellent framework for achieving the objectives of:

- Integrating metrics with the business strategy as part of a "management system"

- Achieving "connectivity" between top-level strategic business goals and lower-level process metrics

- Providing a dynamic systems view based on cause-and-effect relationships of the system

One of the key aspects of the Balanced Scorecard approach is the integration of financial and nonfinancial metrics:

"The collision between the irresistible force to build long-range competitive capabilities and the immovable object of the historical-cost financial accounting model has created a new synthesis: the Balanced Scorecard. The Balanced Scorecard retains traditional financial measures. But financial measures tell the story of past events, an inadequate story for industrial age companies for which investments in long-term capabilities and customer relationships were not critical for success.

"The Balanced Scorecard complements financial measures of performance with measures of the drivers of future performance. The objectives and measures of the scorecard are derived from an organization's vision and strategy. The objectives and measures view organizational performance from four perspectives: financial, customer, internal business process, and learning and growth. These four perspectives provide the framework for the Balanced Scorecard."[9]

The Balanced Scorecard approach also builds on the concept of the "Learning Organization" by providing an objective way to assess the effectiveness of the company's strategy and its implementation. A more integrated system of metrics provides more direct, real-time feedback and enables companies to take corrective action more rapidly to optimize their strategies and react to changes in the market.

An Example of Balanced Scorecard Metrics

It is important that the strategy and vision be specific and challenge the organization to not only improve existing processes but go beyond the limits of existing processes as well. The goals and objectives should be quantified as much as possible with metrics to:

- Translate the context described by the strategy and vision into actionable results and help build consensus and common understanding of the goals and objectives among all employees.

"We are inflexible not because individuals are locked into fixed ways of operating, but because no one has an understanding of how individual tasks combine to create a result, an understanding absolutely necessary for changing how results are created. We do not provide unsatisfactory service because employees are hostile to customers, but because no employee has the information or perspective needed to explain to customers the status of the process whose results they await."[10]

- Provide feedback to validate/invalidate the assumptions behind the company's strategy and evaluate the effectiveness of its execution so that corrective actions can be taken.

One of the most important aspects of developing an effective system of metrics is to be able to connect metrics at any level throughout the company. Ideally, managers should be able to see the linkage from top-level overall business metrics with customer satisfaction measurements and measures of process performance.

Figure 5.3 provides a model and framework that shows the relationships of the internal process metrics to customer satisfaction metrics and overall business results:

- The top-level process metrics should be sufficient to provide a direct indication of the areas most likely to impact customer value as well as overall performance of the process against other specific requirements.

- Internal process metrics should include more detailed diagnostic metrics to provide the ability to analyze the components of process performance.

The metrics might also include:

- Measurements of employee skills and knowledge (referred to as "learning and growth" metrics in the Balanced Scorecard). For example, many companies neglect to measure the effectiveness of training programs in achieving their desired result. Training effectiveness can be measured at several points. The most obvious place to measure it would be to test the employee's knowledge at the end of the course. A less obvious way to evaluate it would be to determine if there was any improvement in effectiveness after the employee had been back on the job for some period of time.

- Progress metrics that indicate the speed and effectiveness of change and improvement initiatives in the organization in addition to metrics of current process performance. This requires a balance of emphasis on short-term operational performance metrics as well as longer-term strategic progress metrics.

The Role of Customer Value Measurement

Customer value is the key element in the Balanced Scorecard that integrates the whole model around a unifying direction. Analyzing customer values

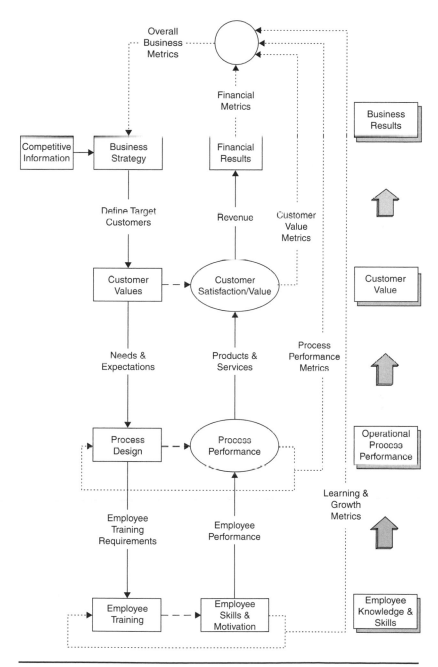

Figure 5.3 Alignment of business metrics.

and competition and defining a value proposition that will uniquely position the company to satisfy those needs is a critical part of fully implementing a Balanced Scorecard approach. No company can succeed today by trying to be all things to all people.

The business strategy should define what specific customer segments the company is focused on and how the company will differentiate its unique value-added to those customers relative to the competition. Once that is done, a customer value analysis can be done to provide data to support the business strategy and to translate it into specific measurable objectives and metrics for measuring progress.

Customer value measurement is broader than customer satisfaction measurement. Customer value measurement is focused on identifying the drivers of customer behavior that influence the company's business results and measure the perception of the company and its products and services by the customer against those factors. Customer satisfaction is one component of that measurement. Example drivers of customer behavior that would influence business results include factors that influence:

- The initial purchase decision

- Repurchasing additional products and services from the same company

- Referring the company's products and services to others

In most cases, customer satisfaction measures the satisfaction of the customer after they have purchased the product and does not necessarily attempt to link it to business results. For example, factors that influence initial purchase behavior, such as the perception of the company relative to its competitors, might be outside the scope of a typical customer satisfaction measurement.

Customer value measurement is a very broad topic and it is not the intent of this book to try to cover it completely; however, here are some things to consider in developing an approach to measuring and managing customer value:

1. Customer Segmentation

    It is very important to consider whether the company's customer base is homogeneous or not. If a customer base is very diverse, measuring the entire customer base as an aggregate may give misleading results because it masks some of the differences within the base of customers.

Another factor to consider is that within a customer account there are a variety of people who influence or make purchasing decisions, and each of them may have different motivations.

2. The Role of a Qualitative Survey

A mistake many companies make is to measure what they *think* is important to the customer and they may either overlook something the customer considers important that they are not aware of or place undue importance on something that has very low importance to the customer. An approach to resolve this is to combine a qualitative survey with a quantitative survey. The objective of the qualitative survey would be to identify the factors that are important to the customer as a first step prior to performing a quantitative survey and analysis. The role of the quantitative survey would be to measure the customer's perception of the company and its products and services against those factors that were identified in the qualitative survey.

One approach to performing a qualitative survey is to do a focus group where a number of customers are invited to attend a discussion that is typically moderated by a third party and sometimes done anonymously so that the company sponsoring the event does not overly influence or bias the outcome. The customers are asked to discuss their perceptions of products, services, companies, and the factors that motivate their decisions. This approach is commonly used in consumer goods, where very subtle factors such as the color of a box on the grocery shelf might be a factor in the consumer's purchase decision.

3. The Importance of Competitive Data

Absolute measurements of customer satisfaction do not necessarily tell the whole story. The best approach is to combine it with equivalent data of a competitor to understand the company's perception relative to the competition.

It is very important to design a good methodology for measuring customer value and customer satisfaction. Unless it is implemented consistently over a period of time, it will be extremely difficult—if not impossible—to identify trends. For example, changing the measurement approach or the measurement factors too frequently might make it very difficult to tell if the company is improving or not. *Managing Customer Value* by Brad Gale describes a quantifiable method for performing a customer value analysis in more detail.[11]

Ideally, the results of the value analysis and the business strategy should drive an action plan to improve internal process performance; and, in turn, define the critical infrastructure (employee knowledge and skills as well as supporting IT systems) that the organization must build to succeed.

Balanced Scorecard Summary

The Balanced Scorecard is an idealized model and it is rarely fully implemented in actual practice. For example, it may not be feasible to develop a precise and quantitative measurement of customer value as this example presents, and it may not be possible to exactly understand the linkages between the various levels in the model. Nonetheless, it is a useful concept to understand how the overall system works as well as the general interrelationship of its various elements. Jack Steele identifies 10 steps that should be included in the complete implementation of a Balanced Scorecard approach:[12]

- Development of a solid strategy

- Translation of a strategy into a scorecard of clear objectives

- Attachment of measures to each objective

- Cascading of scorecards to the front line (hierarchical linkages of metrics)

- Alignment of existing core processes to objectives

- Delivery of measurement-based performance feedback

- Accountability of people for performance measures

- Empowerment of work groups to implement improvement initiatives

- Linkage of initiatives to the budgeting process

- Reassessment of the main strategy

THE ROLE OF METRICS

Using Metrics to Achieve Cross-Functional Integration

In addition to the role of metrics in achieving vertical alignment (linking business results with customer value metrics and linking customer value metrics with process metrics), metrics also can play a very important role in achieving horizontal integration (integration across functions within the organization).

I worked for a very large electronics company in the early 1990s and quality managers frequently received directives from the corporate quality organization saying something like, "We want you to go over to the operational management groups and get them to improve their product quality (or some other measurement)." These directives came down through the quality chain of command and, in many cases, there was absolutely nothing that supported it that came through the operational management chain of command. I am sure many quality managers recognize this immediately as a familiar situation because it happens all the time. The result is obvious: the quality manager has to beg, plead, cajole, coerce, or use whatever other means he/she has at his/her disposal to try to get this done.

That is a very inefficient use of resources and the solution is easy—just giving the operational managers themselves a direct metric with goals will accomplish the same thing much more efficiently. If that happens, it changes the ball game entirely. Now the operational managers have the primary responsibility to get this done, and instead of the quality manager wasting time to push on getting it done, it happens much more "automatically." The role of the quality manager also shifts; instead of being an enforcer, he/she becomes a value-added process consultant. Now the operational manager has the primary responsibility to get it done and is "pulling" on the quality management function for help in figuring out how to get it done. The result is a much more efficient use of resources. By putting the primary responsibility on the people who have direct control of the outcome, the solution is also likely to be much more effective as well.

Using Metrics for Benchmarking and Goal Setting

TL 9000 is the telecommunications industry implementation of the ISO 9000 family of standards. TL 9000 has recognized the important role that metrics play in a good quality management system and it requires mandatory reporting of standardized metrics to an industry data repository managed by the University of Texas at Dallas (UTD). Metrics play a very important role in the TL 9000 standard by.

- Putting "teeth" in the standard and providing an objective measurement of whether any real improvement is taking place

- Providing a common framework of communication between the customer and the supplier to set mutually agreed-upon goals for continuous improvement

TL 9000 standardizes the definition of the metrics so that everyone in the industry who reports metrics counts the data and reports it in a consistent way. UTD publishes statistical results of the metrics to allow companies to compare their own performance to industry norms, which provides an automated form of benchmarking and a built-in incentive for continuous improvement.

The following are some points to keep in mind to design an effective system of metrics:

1. Metrics without goals are just interesting data.

    Many companies fall into the trap of collecting huge amounts of data for all kinds of metrics and never set goals to do anything with the data.

2. A good system of metrics should have structure and should be hierarchical in nature.

    It is very easy to overwhelm people with too much data—to the point that it becomes difficult to really draw any conclusions from it:

    •   A good metrics system should have some higher-level indicators that are analogous to the "dashboard" on a car. They tell you at a glance how the most important things are going without too much detail.

    •   However, the metrics system must also provide the ability to "drill down" for more detail as necessary to analyze what's going on when there's a problem.

    At the lowest level, the data should provide sufficient granularity to support process improvement initiatives to analyze the root cause of problems. For example, the high-level data would probably show an aggregate such as the increasing total number of problem reports. That data has very limited granularity and probably provides insufficient detail for further analyzing the problem. What you would probably like to have to supplement it is a higher level of granularity to show more details for further analysis, such as a pattern in the data by product, by type of problem, by customer, et cetera.

3. A time orientation is very important.

    •   Provide a measure of past trends to determine if there is an improvement or degradation in results and to determine if progress is consistent with achieving goals.

- Provide, as well, an advance indicator of future events. For example, a significant increase in the number of customer problem reports is probably an advance indicator of a decline in customer satisfaction, which may ultimately lead to lost business revenue.

4. Benchmark comparison data is extremely valuable.

   Some companies make the mistake of tracking only their own results and fail to benchmark themselves against competitors and best-in-class results. That can lead to an illusion that the company is doing well when, in fact, it is not.

Linking Strategy to Execution

Metrics is one of the most important tools available to create an integrated environment that supports continuous improvement. People are motivated by metrics and well-designed systems of metrics can be a very important unifying and integrating force in any company. The Balanced Scorecard model creates an environment for integrating business and process management objectives around a common focus of customer value generation, and for facilitating and sustaining incremental as well as radical process improvement efforts. Implementing a sound strategic planning process with appropriate metrics to monitor progress will provide the framework to identify and prioritize areas for improvement, and to keep those efforts aligned with the overall strategy.

> ". . . the ability to implement large-scale change is only part of the solution. The challenge is finding ways to keep on doing it and building into the organization the capacity to continually transform itself."[13]

The Balanced Scorecard is a great concept; unfortunately, it is sometimes implemented as a "program" and there is an attempt to redefine the whole company around a Balanced Scorecard approach. It is only a tool that needs to be used in combination with other approaches to design and implement effective management systems. It also is not necessary to fully implement the Balanced Scorecard to gain benefit from the concepts behind it. Just having an understanding of the cause-and-effect relationships among metrics in a business is helpful to better understand the operation of the business.

AN EXAMPLE—CESSNA AIRCRAFT

When Michael R. Katzorke, Senior Vice President of Supply Chain Management at Cessna Aircraft Company in Wichita, Kansas began working on the company's supply chain management system in 1998, Cessna was still a traditional aerospace firm. It had a functional orientation, was vertically integrated, had traditional processes and practices, and there was no provision for total quality management or Six Sigma.[14]

Cessna adopted a new vision for the 21st century called "Cessna 20/20." Its business model focuses on processes and their linkages (as opposed to traditional, functional, hierarchical models). Its vision, as summarized by its "High Five" objectives is:[15]

- Total customer satisfaction

- World quality standard for aviation

- Breakthrough operating performance

- Top-10 companies to work for in America

- Superior financial performance

Cessna defines its supply chain as "from ore in the ground to product obsolescence." The supply chain process translates the "High Five" objectives to the following goals for its supply chain:[16]

- Improve quality/reliability 10-fold in three years

- Improve annual productivity in terms of cost, not inflation

- Improve on-time delivery 10-fold in three years

- Improve cycle time threefold in three years

Some of the early results of this effort include:[17]

- Quality: ~30X Improvement

- Reliability: Product support agreement alignment with customer desires

- Schedule: 28 percent improvement (99 percent on-time consistently)

- Productivity: Escalation largely replaced by productivity

- Production Inventory: Production turns increased 3 times

ENDNOTES

1. T. H. Davenport, *Process Innovation* (Cambridge, MA: Harvard Business School Press, 1993): 117–18.
2. J. Collins, *Good to Great* (New York: HarperCollins, 2001): 91.
3. Ibid.
4. Ibid., 95–96.
5. http://www.sprint.com/sprint/values/quality/.
6. B. Sheehy, H. Bracey, and R. Frazier, *Winning the Race for Value* (New York: American Management Association, 1996): 145.
7. Ibid., 102.
8. R. S. Kaplan and D. P. Norton, *The Balanced Scorecard* (Cambridge, MA: Harvard Business School Press, 1996).
9. Ibid., 7–8.
10. M. Hammer, *Beyond Reengineering* (New York: HarperCollins, 1996): 6.
11. B. T. Gale, *Managing Customer Value* (New York: Free Press, 1994): 28–35.
12. J. Steele, "Transforming the Balanced Scorecard into Your Strategy Execution System," *Manage* (September/October 2001).
13. I. Somerville and J. E. Mroz, "New Competencies for a New World," in *The Organization of the Future* (San Francisco: Jossey-Bass, 1997): 76.
14. "Cessna aims to drive SCM to its very core," *Purchasing* (June 6, 2002): 31–35.
15. Ibid.
16. Ibid.
17. Ibid.

6

Integrated Process Improvement Approach

CHAPTER OVERVIEW

In addition to having a well-defined model of how the business works, it is also essential to have a methodology for continuous improvement on an ongoing basis that includes provisions for both incremental improvement as well as more radical reengineering, if it is required.

A number of different improvement methodologies have been competing with each other for some time. Although Six Sigma is gaining widespread support because of its success at General Electric, it is important to understand the capabilities and limitations of Six Sigma as well as other methodologies. An understanding of the fundamental logic behind these methodologies will enable creating a more integrated approach and enable using each of them more effectively in the right context.

In this chapter, we will discuss a number of different process improvement methodologies. It is very easy to get lost in the implementation details of each of these methodologies and lose sight of the fundamental requirements that should be common to all of them. Any effective process improvement approach should include the following essential elements:

1. Strong Emphasis on Problem Analysis

   An analysis of the problem or opportunity for improvement to determine root cause to ensure that the solution is a true systemic fix and not just a "band-aid" to fix an instance of a problem that is only going to reappear somewhere else.

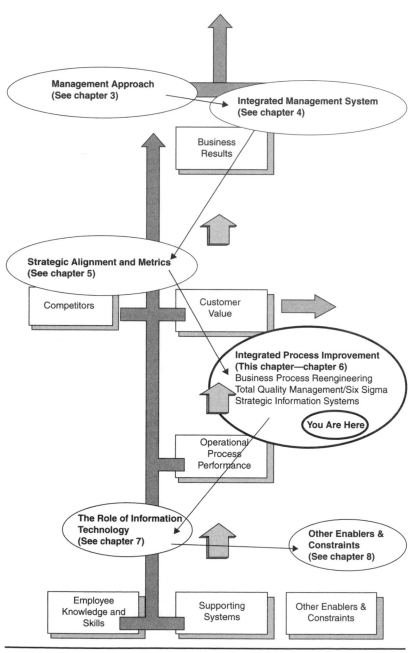

This navigational roadmap is intended to help readers understand the flow of information in these chapters and see how various topics fit into the overall model.

2. System Solution Approach

   A solutions approach that takes into consideration interrelated functions of the system so that fixing one problem does not cause another problem to appear in another area.

3. Sound Project Management Methodology

   A good project management methodology to ensure that process improvement initiatives are completed successfully and achieve their objectives.

4. Validation Approach

   A way of validating that the solution was effective and some way of measuring the effectiveness of the solution.

5. Portfolio Management Approach

   In a large company with a major process improvement program like Six Sigma, there can be a significant number of these initiatives going on. Prioritizing potential opportunities for improvement, as well as keeping them all coordinated and focused on the company's goals, can be a major challenge.

TOTAL QUALITY MANAGEMENT

The American Society for Quality (ASQ) defines total quality management (TQM) as follows:

"TQM is a business philosophy related to an organization's management system that:

- Seeks to improve the results, including the financial performance
- Guarantees long-term survival through a consistent focus on improving customer satisfaction
- Meets the needs of all its stakeholders (customers, employees, owners, and suppliers)

"Overall, TQM:

- Institutionalizes a never-ending process of improvement
- Emphasizes and is driven by the need to meet and exceed customer needs and expectations

- Works to eliminate waste and rework
- Harnesses the brainpower of all people in the organization

"Further, TQM focuses on:

- External factors including the customer, competition, and society
- Management leadership and commitment
- Employee participation and empowerment
- Sensitivity to the needs of internal and external customers
- Continuous improvement of processes, products, and services
- Fact-based decision making

"The critical aspects of TQM are its customer orientation, its emphasis on continuous improvement, and its organizationwide aspects—the participation of all members of the organization aiming, together, at long-term success through customer satisfaction.

"Process management embraces a systems approach to management and a holistic view of the organization. An organization is seen as a unified, purposeful system composed of interrelated processes. Instead of dealing with functional activities, process management advocates managing the system by process hierarchy—across boundaries as the work gets done."[1]

Evolution of Total Quality Management Philosophy

The total quality management (TQM) philosophy originated from the ideas of Dr. W. Edwards Deming and others. Dr. Deming was an American statistician credited with the rise of Japan as a manufacturing nation. Dr. Deming's original 14 points are the basis for the TQM philosophy:[2]

1. Create constancy of purpose toward improvement of products and services with the aim of becoming competitive, staying in business, and providing jobs.

2. Adopt the new philosophy.

"Western management must awaken to the challenge, learn their responsibilities, and provide leadership to change the situation.

3. Cease dependence on inspection by building quality into the product in the first place.

4. Move toward a single supplier for any one item.

End the practice of awarding contracts to the lowest bidder. Move toward a single supplier for any one item and build a long-term relationship of loyalty and trust. Cheaper is not always better.

5. Improve constantly and forever.

Constantly improve quality and productivity in order to constantly decrease costs.

6. Institute training on the job.

Employee training is an important aspect of a quality system that is often overlooked.

7. Institute leadership.

Supervision should help people and machines do a better job. Supervision of management is in need of overhaul as well as supervision of production workers.

8. Drive out fear so that everyone may work effectively for the company.

9. Break down barriers between departments.

People in research, design, sales, and production must work as a team.

10. Eliminate slogans, exhortations, and targets for the workforce, such as asking for zero defects. Such exhortations only create adversarial relationships, since most of the causes of low quality and low productivity are in the system and are beyond the control of the workforce.

11. Eliminate management by objectives.

Eliminate management by the numbers and numerical goals. Substitute leadership.

12. Remove barriers to pride of workmanship.

The responsibility of supervisors must be changed from sheer numbers to quality.

13. Institute education and self-improvement.

Institute a vigorous program of education and self-improvement.

14. The transformation is everyone's job.

Put everyone in the company to work to accomplish the transformation—through quality control circles, for example.

However, because there were a number of leaders in the TQM movement in addition to Dr. Deming (Juran, Ishikawa, Feigenbaum, and many others) and Dr. Deming intentionally chose to focus on defining key principles and not a prescriptive approach, TQM is somewhat loosely defined.

Dr. Deming intentionally wanted managers to take the time to interpret what those principles mean to their business rather than giving them a canned methodology. That is exactly why the implementation of more prescriptive standards, such as ISO 9000, is many times so weak. Companies often do not take time to interpret what it means to their business and how they can use it to improve the effectiveness of the business. Most of Dr. Deming's points are still fundamentally sound today, although they may need some adjustment to fit today's environment.

TQM is based heavily on systems thinking. Instead of focusing on trying to control the result of a process alone, Dr. Deming taught us to focus on the causal factors within the overall system that impact and influence the result. It is far more effective to design processes and systems that prevent defects from occurring altogether, rather than relying on corrective measures to detect and correct defects that have already occurred.

The implementation of total quality management in the United States was generally associated with bringing about widespread cultural change that was necessary in the 1980s and early 1990s, because at that time American quality was seriously deficient relative to the Japanese. The biggest impact of TQM was to increase the level of understanding of the cultural change and other broad-based requirements needed to improve quality.

Table 6.1 illustrates only a few of the key successes that have come from the TQM movement.

The one point out of the 14 original points that has caused the most controversy is number 11, "Eliminate management by objectives." Many people became disenchanted with TQM because there was insufficient focus on producing measurable results. However, all of the other points in TQM are still generally sound and have made a significant contribution to creating a broader understanding of a systems approach to improving quality.

TQM Improvement Methodology

TQM emphasizes ongoing, continuous improvement based on a structured problem-solving approach. There is no well-defined or prescribed improvement methodology for TQM. The following is an example of a TQM problem-solving approach used by Sprint. (This information is reproduced with permission of Sprint from the Sprint Quality Handbook . . . a complete and more detailed copy of the entire Sprint Quality System Handbook is available online at http://www.sprint.com/sprint/values/quality/sprint_quality_handbook.pdf.)

Table 6.1   Examples of impact of Dr. Deming's 14 points.

Key Area of Impact	Deming's Original Point
The way to improve quality is not to increase the level of inspection, it is to remove sources of variation from the process and the production system. Ideally, that eliminates the need for inspection altogether. This is the principle that Six Sigma is based on and it is the fundamental principle of a systems approach to quality management.	"Cease dependence on inspection" (Point #3).
The importance of leadership and the distinction between leadership and management.	"Institute leadership" (Point #7).
Successful implementation requires widespread buy-in and participation throughout the company (it is not just the job of the quality control department).	• "Adopt the new philosophy" (Point #2). • "The transformation is everyone's job" (Point #14).
The importance of tightly integrated supply chains.	"Move toward a single supplier for any one item" (Point #4).
The need for cross-functional collaboration.	"Break down barriers between departments" (Point #9).
Emphasis on the human aspects of quality. • Importance of training • Pride of workmanship • Employee engagement and participation	• "Institute training on the job" (Point #6). • "Eliminate barriers to pride of workmanship" (Point #5). • "Drive out fear" (Point #8). • "Institute education and self-improvement" (Point #13).

An Example—Sprint Process Improvement Methodology

Sprint has developed and implemented a process improvement approach based on the TQM principles, which has been implemented throughout the company. The major steps in the Sprint approach are:

1. Reason for Improvement

   Identify the general problem area (the "theme") and the reason for working on it. Key questions to ask include:

   • What do we do (for example, what work/products do we produce)?

- For whom do we do it (who is our customer)?

- How well are we doing (what is our customer's view)?

- How do we know (what is our indicator)?

2. Problem Identification

   Select a specific problem from the general problem area (the "theme") identified in step 1 and set a target for improvement. Step 2, combined with step 1, enables us to focus on a specific problem rather than a broad area. Having this focus will make it easier to determine root causes in step 3.

3. Root Cause Analysis

   Identify and verify the root causes of the specific problem identified in step 2. Root cause analysis will be easier to do if the problem has been significantly narrowed in steps 1 and 2.

4. Potential Improvements

   Plan improvements that will correct the root causes identified in step 3, then test these improvements on a small scale.

5. Verification

   Verify that you have reduced a problem, its root causes, and/or improved a process, and confirm that you have met the target for improvement. If what you tried didn't work or didn't work as well as you expected, study what worked and what didn't work, and go through steps 3 and 4 again.

6. Full Implementation

   Prevent the problem and its root causes from recurring. Implement the improvements wherever possible.

7. Future Plans

   Plan what to do about any remaining problems. Evaluate the effectiveness of the problem-solving process, including the effectiveness of the team.

Any methodology like this is only a management framework and provides guidelines for successful implementation. It requires skilled people to implement it effectively and Sprint offers a number of courses through its "University of Excellence" to support this approach.

BUSINESS PROCESS REENGINEERING

Business Process Reengineering Overview

Reengineering, or more specifically, business process reengineering (BPR), was originally defined by Michael Hammer and James Champy as:

> "The *fundamental* rethinking and *radical* redesign of the business *processes* to achieve *dramatic* improvements in critical, contemporary measures of performance . . ."[3]

Each of the keywords in this definition is explained in Table 6.2.

The "reengineering movement" as we knew it in the 1990s is over; however, that is typically a reaction to how "reengineering" has been implemented in actual practice, not the concept behind it. The revolutionary

Table 6.2   Keywords in reengineering definition.

Fundamental	Reengineering is "fundamental" insofar as we must ask the most basic questions about the company and how it operates, such as, "Why are we doing something the way it is done?" Too often, effort is spent fixing a process without thinking why the process is there in the first place, and whether it needs to be there at all.
Radical	Reengineering is also "radical." This does not mean that reengineering must be revolutionary or violent; rather, what it means is that we must focus on the "root" of the problems. (As Michael Hammer likes to point out, "radical" shares its etymology with the word "radish," one of the better-known roots.) Reengineering involves a reinventing of processes by focusing on their roots and is willing to consider completely redesigning the process or eliminating it altogether if necessary to improve effectiveness.
Dramatic	Reengineering is required when you need dramatic improvements. Marginal improvements, such as a 10% improvement in the cycle time of a process or a 5% cut in costs, do not require reengineering. Techniques such as quality initiatives or process improvement will often suffice in those cases.
Process	Process redesigns drive reengineering efforts, not tasks, jobs, or organizations. Historically, management focused on individual, narrowly defined tasks and jobs (for example, how to best capture a customer's merchandise order). We need to shift the emphasis toward a collection of these tasks that provide value to the customer.

rhetoric with which reengineering was originally promoted and the brute force approach with which it has been many times implemented has unfortunately given it a bad reputation; however, the underlying principles behind it are sound.

There is very certainly a need for ongoing process improvement; however, limiting the scope of those improvements to more gradual incremental improvements without fundamentally rethinking the processes as well as the organizations and systems associated with them will produce only limited results in many cases. What is needed is an integrated approach for *both* incremental as well as radical process improvement—and it is actually very easy to integrate these two approaches.

Complex Improvement and Reengineering Methodology

One of the reasons the reengineering movement came about was due to the enabling impact of new information technology. In many situations, the use of information technology enabled major breakthroughs in the way things were done in business processes.

A good example of that is in product distribution. Prior to the reengineering movement in the early 1990s, it was common for companies to have large distribution networks with numerous warehouses all containing substantial amounts of inventory in order to provide an effective level of service to their customers. Rethinking of that overall process from the perspective of the overall supply chain and the advent of "just in time" delivery schemes caused some radical redefinition of that whole process.

If you are a supplier to Wal-Mart, for example, you are expected to deliver your product directly to their loading dock within a very narrow window of time that might only be a few hours. The benefits of this approach are obvious:

- The delivery goes right from the truck onto the display shelf for sale. There are no intermediate distribution centers or storerooms in the stores to hold inventory, which dramatically improves inventory turns.

- People can be more precisely scheduled to do the unloading and stocking of the material as needed without extensive idle time waiting for it to arrive, which improves utilization of personnel and reduces unnecessary costs.

- Huge savings in real estate and property management costs result from "blowing away" the warehouses, storerooms, and distribution centers that might have been needed.

Of course, none of this would be possible without tight coordination between Wal-Mart and its suppliers and that, of course, cannot be done effectively without a significant use of information technology.

Because they are so broad in scope and involve radical rethinking of processes with significant amounts of information technology, reengineering projects are typically very high risk. They also may have significant impact from a human resources perspective and might require a significant amount of change management, training, and reorientation of employees for the new approach to be accepted, which, of course, further increases the risk. Some of the additional risks and challenges this causes are:

1. Translating the business requirements into software development and system requirements

   Successful implementation requires an approach that connects the implementation of the systems with the design of the business processes they are designed to support. Many IT solutions have gone astray implementing a technical solution that was not well connected with the business problems it was designed to solve.

2. All of the normal risks associated with any software development effort (managing the scope, mitigating the risks, and so on)

   Software development efforts are well known for being full of risks that need to be carefully managed.

3. Keeping the software development effort and systems development effort in synch with the other aspects of the project

   A team is typically needed. In many situations, no single individual has all the skills required to define and implement the complete solution. The roles all of the members of the team need to be defined in the context of an overall project lifecycle model to provide a framework for successfully orchestrating the definition, design, and implementation of the solution.

4. Anticipating all the areas of impact of the reengineering and effectively managing changes

   This is probably one of the biggest areas of risk because some of the areas of impact may not be obvious and the impact may be significant.

For these reasons, successful implementation of a major reengineering initiative requires careful planning and a well-designed methodology that considers all aspects of potential impact of the project implementation; the methodology should provide an effective mechanism for managing the risk. Even though reengineering does typically involve a much higher level of risk than a more gradual, incremental improvement approach, there are many situations where reengineering is an essential approach to consider:

- Incremental improvement efforts that focus on gradual improvement within a process rarely consider radical redesign or replacement of the process and might overlook significant benefits that could result from doing it completely differently.

- It is becoming increasingly difficult to separate the design of the business processes from the information systems associated with those processes. Any significant software development or information systems effort that might be required to complete an improvement initiative can dramatically increase its complexity. As a result, it may require a reengineering approach rather than an incremental improvement approach to effectively manage the risk and changes involved. In many situations, the rewards of introducing new technology to improve a process can far outweigh the risks.

Appendix A contains an example lifecycle model that can be used to integrate complex process improvement projects for reengineering efforts or other complex improvement initiatives. These initiatives may be limited in scope and easy to implement or much broader, more complex, and difficult to implement. The model starts with developing an understanding of the company's business requirements and works down from there progressively into the definition, design, and implementation of a solution to help improve the customer's business. There are several very important aspects of this model:

- It does not start with the goal of implementing a particular software application or information system. Ideally, it starts with a clean slate in an attempt to understand the company's business needs and goals.

- It attempts to bridge the gap between the IT technological perspective and a business and operations perspective, and in many cases will require cross-functional buy-in and support from different organizations within the company's business.

- There is much more effort required to identify and define company business requirements as well as potential solutions because the solution is assumed to be much broader and more complex.

- It typically requires a team of people to implement the whole approach.

- Clearly defined roles and responsibilities, well-orchestrated communications, excellent project management, and appropriate review points in the project are essential to manage the overall project.

The intent of this model is to show one possible approach to organizing a project for defining and implementing complex system solutions. In reading or using this model, it is important to understand that this is only a model and not the *only* potential model for doing this. The important points to be considered are:

- The model can be entered at different points. The normal starting point is an understanding of the business requirements. If the company already feels confident that the business requirements are understood, the model can be entered at a later stage.

- The roles identified in this model are hypothetical. In the simplest case, many of them might be combined as needed (one person might perform several different roles).

- The complexity of the model needs to be adjusted so that it is appropriate to the risks, scope, and complexity of the overall effort.

Relationship of TQM and Reengineering

In the 1990s, reengineering and total quality management (TQM) were sometimes seen as competitive because different groups of people strongly advocated each approach, but they were actually very complementary:

- A radical process reengineering initiative probably will not succeed unless there is an ongoing process improvement approach in place to sustain any gains.

- An incremental process improvement effort will have limited success if it doesn't consider the possibility of more radical changes as a potential solution.

The major differences between TQM and reengineering were not in the methodology itself but in the scope of change that would normally be considered. Both reengineering and TQM efforts also need to be connected into the company's business strategy to define and prioritize areas for improvement. Rather than approaching a problem from either a reengineering or TQM perspective, the right approach is to approach it from a business strategy perspective and consider the relative advantages of both approaches for the particular initiative.

There is no reason why a consistent management process cannot be applied to both, although there will likely be considerable differences in the scope and complexity of decisions as well as implementation requirements. The complementary nature of these two approaches was finally being recognized in the late 1990s. Michael Hammer's book *Beyond Reengineering* suggested that process-centered organizations will become the dominant force in business and now recognizes that, "Reengineering and TQM are merely different pews in the church of process improvement."[4] Barry Sheehy expresses it much more directly:

> "Reengineering and CPI [TQM] are just different points along the same continuum. To start one is to begin the other. The polarization caused by the reengineering vs. CPI debate was harmful and distracting. The whole fuss was about as relevant to the real economy as the annual fashion debates about hemlines. The overblown rhetoric surrounding such tools as reengineering creates an obstacle to learning. The supposed dichotomy between CPI and innovation was never real, at least as it applies to existing business processes. For an organization seeking to improve, it is not a case of choosing one over the other, but of pursuing one or both when they make sense. Teams which set out to incrementally improve processes very often break through and achieve dramatic results. Inversely, breakthrough teams searching for dramatic improvement often fall short and only achieve incremental results. Either way, things get better."[5]

Figure 6.1 shows the relationship of a continuous improvement approach (TQM) and a reengineering approach. A well-integrated improvement methodology should consider both.

- Limiting an improvement methodology to an incremental approach, without considering the possibility of major redefinition of processes where it makes sense, might lead to ignoring very large opportunities for improvement and wasting time on tweaking an existing process that should be replaced altogether.

- Focusing on reengineering alone without considering the need for ongoing continuous improvement has led reengineering projects to fail because no mechanism was in place to sustain and continue the results of the reengineering effort.

Figure 6.2 shows a timeline of how reengineering and continuous improvement (TQM) might be integrated in the life of a process or business system. At key points in the evolution of the process there might be a need

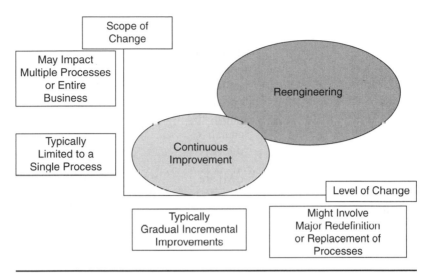

Figure 6.1   Relationship between reengineering and continuous improvement.

for major reengineering to take advantage of new technology, new methods, and new ideas about how to perform the process more effectively. Between those points, however, there is a need for continuous improvement to sustain the results of the reengineering effort and to introduce other incremental improvements.

Both TQM and reengineering had some value that we can learn from. The principles behind TQM were very sound; however, as with other quality "programs," the implementation went astray in a number of instances:

- In many cases, the primary focus of TQM initiatives was bringing about a cultural change in the company with an increased focus on quality and customer satisfaction. Although it did accomplish that in many situations, there was an insufficient level of focus on quantifiable results.

- In other cases, numerous TQM efforts have not been well aligned with the company's business goals.

When I worked for a large electronics company in the early 1990s, we had a very broad-based TQM program called *total customer satisfaction* (TCS) where teams competed with each other to develop the best quality improvement initiative. There was much "hoopla" associated with it and it definitely had a big impact on improving the culture of the company, but one of the most difficult aspects of managing the program was keeping it

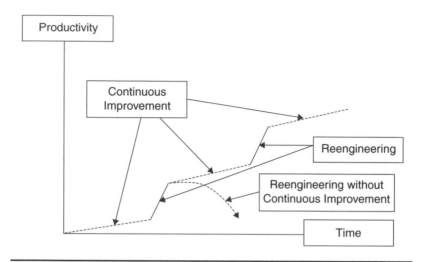

Figure 6.2 Integration of reengineering with continuous improvement.

focused and keeping it aligned with measurable results that were important to the company's business strategy.

It was a "grass roots," bottom-up kind of initiative—anyone in the company down to all of the people on the manufacturing floor could put together a team to focus on a TCS improvement initiative. Teams competed with each other, and the winning team won a significant prize, such as a trip to Bali, Indonesia. While many of these efforts were worthwhile, it was difficult to keep it well aligned with the company's business strategy, and couple it with the broader and strategic initiatives that were driven by senior management. Teams would spring up to try to cut costs of using paper in copying machines, for example.

One of the biggest things to be gained from TQM-style initiatives was the focus on creating a customer-focused culture and empowering people at all levels to improve customer satisfaction. The lesson that can be learned from some of the implementation efforts is that it must be focused and measured quantifiably to ensure that it produces appropriate business results, and effective project management needs to be applied to ensure TQM initiatives produce the appropriate results. Although TQM might be viewed as something that is "out of style" today, many of the principles behind it are still very sound and the cultural aspects of it are something that we should not lose sight of.

Probably the biggest contribution of the reengineering movement was that it encouraged people to "think outside the box" and to look for radically different ways of doing things. The way it was typically implemented, however, was competitive with TQM. There was little sensitivity to the employee morale and cultural impacts of some of the brute force, "slash-and-burn" reengineering efforts. There was also inadequate recognition of the need to provide a way for ongoing incremental improvement after the reengineering effort was done.

Both TQM and reengineering may be viewed as passé today, but even though they may not be in vogue as a "program," there are valuable aspects of both approaches that are still worthwhile that we should not lose sight of. The tendency, however, is to "throw the baby out with the bath water" and start over again from scratch with an entirely different methodology.

SIX SIGMA

Six Sigma has emerged as a logical successor to the TQM and reengineering movements of the 1990s. It is consistent with the overall goals of TQM, but puts more emphasis on achieving focused and quantifiable results. Six Sigma has two major connotations:

- A measure of defects in a process—In this context, a Six Sigma process has approximately 3.4 defects per million opportunities.

- A methodology and a problem-solving approach for process improvement—In this context, Six Sigma defines a disciplined approach for defining, measuring, analyzing, improving, and controlling process improvement initiatives.

These two contexts were directly related at one time. Six Sigma has typically been focused on reduction of defects in a process, and the methodology was originally developed by Motorola as a way of getting to Six Sigma levels of defects in processes and products. That is how the Six Sigma methodology got its name; however, those two contexts are not necessarily related.

The Six Sigma methodology is really a very sound problem-solving process that can be extended to a much wider range of situations which are not necessarily associated with reduction of defects in a process, and do not necessarily have a goal of reaching a Six Sigma level of defects. The problem resolution also may not require "heavy duty" statistical analysis at all, depending on the goals of the improvement initiative. What's important about Six Sigma is to have a well thought-out methodology for defining, implementing, and sustaining improvement initiatives that can be extended to a full range of problem-solving requirements and process improvement initiatives. The following is a summary of the phases in the Six Sigma methodology (DMAIC):[6]

Define—The project's purpose and scope are defined during this phase and background information on the process and customer is collected. The output of the "Define" phase is a clear statement of the intended improvement, a high-level map of the process, and a list of what is important to the customer.

Measure—The "Measure" phase is intended to focus the improvement effort by gathering information on the current situation. The output of the "Measure" phase is baseline data on current process performance, data that pinpoints problem location or occurrence, and a more focused problem statement.

Analyze—The goal of the "Analyze" phase is to identify root cause(s) and confirm them with data. The output of the "Analyze" phase is a theory that has been tested and confirmed.

Improve—The "Improve" phase is focused on trying out and implementing solutions that address root causes. The output is planned, tested actions that should eliminate or reduce the impact of the identified root cause(s). Additionally, an approach is defined for evaluating the results in the next ("Control") phase.

Control—The "Control" phase is intended to evaluate the solutions that were developed during the "Improve" phase, and to define and implement an approach for maintaining the gains by standardizing the process. The output of the "Control" phase is a before and after analysis, a monitoring system, completed documentation of results, learnings, and recommendations.

There is a tendency to jump on Six Sigma as the next "program du jour" and forget some of the lessons learned from earlier efforts. Six Sigma is an excellent methodology, and *if it is well implemented*, has the potential to overcome the weaknesses of the TQM movement of the 1990s. There are several things to consider in implementing Six Sigma as part of a successfully integrated management and process improvement system:

1. Six Sigma is primarily a methodology for defining and implementing improvement initiatives and it is only a methodology.

   In itself, it does not provide a management system for defining the overall business strategy and keeping all of the Six Sigma initiatives well aligned with achieving those goals.

In some cases, it is used as a cost-reduction tool and organizations within a company are given dollar targets for Six Sigma cost savings. That approach has some benefits, but does not fully utilize the capabilities that Six Sigma offers. To realize the full benefits of Six Sigma requires combining it with a management system that provides the context to integrate various Six Sigma initiatives and creating an environment that is conducive to ongoing process improvement.

Making Six Sigma Last, by George Eckes, defines four steps that are essential to integrating Six Sigma with the company's strategic business objectives and overcoming the inherent resistance in the organization to effectively implementing Six Sigma. (These same factors are required for most process improvement initiatives to be successful.)[7]

- **Demonstrating the need**

This step requires creating a sense of urgency in the organization based on the risks of not implementing Six Sigma and focusing on long-term opportunities to be gained from this management philosophy.

- **Shaping the Vision**

The strategic vision should include a mission statement that crisply defines the strategic vision and goals to be achieved. (See chapter 4 for more detail.)

- **Identifying and Managing Resistance**

Implementation of Six Sigma and most other quality and process improvement initiatives involves a mindset change and perhaps a cultural change within the organization to be successful. Successfully implementing any effort of this kind requires an understanding of the scope and nature of the changes required, and planning to identify and overcome potential sources of resistance.

- **Changing the Systems and Structures of the Organization**

George Eckes identifies a number of organizational systems and structures that are likely to have a direct impact on the successful implementation of a Six Sigma initiative:[8]

- How an organization hires personnel

- How an organization develops their personnel

- How an organization rewards and recognizes their personnel

- How an organization assesses performance

2. Six Sigma is primarily focused on reduction of defects in a process and has a heavy focus on the aspects of a process that are directly measurable.

   There can be a tendency to overlook some of the factors in a process that may not be easily measurable, such as the impact of employee motivation and corporate culture. A hybrid approach that incorporates some of the TQM kind of thinking with the Six Sigma methodology might be very appropriate in these situations.

   Six Sigma is also heavily oriented on reduction of defects; it can be generalized into a broader process improvement methodology but that requires an understanding of the principles that underlie the Six Sigma approach. Like any other methodology, it is not a "magic formula" that guarantees success. The fundamental aspects of Six Sigma that make it successful are:

   - A defined lifecycle model that encourages good project management of improvement initiatives

   - An emphasis on objective analysis of problems

   - A results orientation

3. Six Sigma lends itself more to an incremental improvement approach (like TQM).

   The original definition of Six Sigma was oriented around incremental improvements to a process (like TQM). However, the methodology can be extended to include consideration of more radical process redesign or replacement when it is more appropriate rather than continuously tweaking the current process. The impact of information technology also needs to be considered. Effective use of information technology can dramatically increase the impact of the process improvement initiative, but it also can significantly increase the risk and complexity of the effort and may require a lifecycle model that goes beyond the normal Six Sigma process to effectively manage the risk.

   Raytheon overcomes this weakness by adding a sixth step to the Six Sigma process for "Visualization." According to Don Ronchi,

Vice President of Raytheon Six Sigma, "If you can't visualize your current state, your desired end-state and the gap in-between, you haven't defined your problem properly."[9] Without this additional step, there is a tendency to incrementally improve the current process without considering more radical reengineering that might be a more appropriate solution.

Many project management and process improvement disciplines go astray because people attempt to apply them mechanically without a full understanding of the principles they are based on. Six Sigma is only a guide for developing an effective process improvement approach; as with most other methodologies, there is no substitute for skill and training to apply it effectively.

OTHER IMPROVEMENT METHODOLOGIES

There are other process improvement methodologies that may be appropriate, such as lean manufacturing, and should be considered in developing an integrated process improvement model. However, it is outside of the scope of this book to cover all possible methodologies that might be used.

INTEGRATED IMPROVEMENT APPROACH

Figure 6.3 shows a way these methodologies can be combined into one well-integrated approach.

AN EXAMPLE—MAJOR FINANCIAL SERVICES COMPANY

As an example of a company that has successfully developed an integrated approach to process improvement and process management, a major financial services company became the first company in North America in the financial services industry to achieve ISO 9000 certification. The company used the ISO 9000 criteria as a foundation for a very large process reengineering initiative, resulting in over $57 million in cost reductions and cost avoidance over a two-and-a-half-year period.

A senior-level process management executive was appointed to lead this effort with cross-functional responsibility for integrating all the areas of the organization around achieving these goals, and a senior management

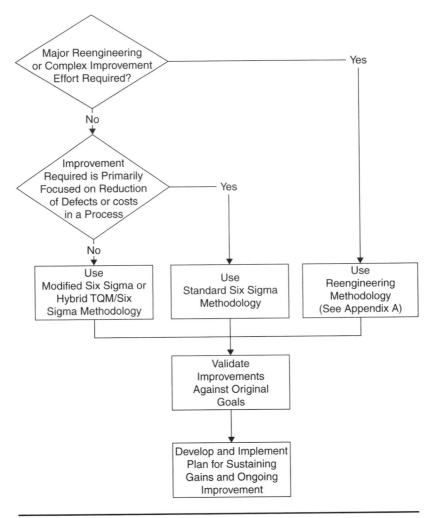

Figure 6.3   Integrated process improvement methodology.

steering committee was charged with providing overall strategic direction and integration with the company's business strategy. There were a number of factors that were significant about this project:

1.   It took a considerable amount of interpretation to apply the criteria in the ISO 9000 standard to a financial services company at the time because it had never been done before in North America. Since that time, a number of other major companies in the financial services industry are now following the lead from this project and are working to define a new stan-

dard called "FS9000" which will be a permanent financial services industry interpretation of the ISO 9000 standard.

2. Prior to the implementation of this project, the company had 25 zones in the field where much of the day-to-day business operations were conducted. Process mapping and auditing were conducted across the entire organization to identify best practices as part of a major reengineering effort, and to standardize and simplify business processes across all of the United States, Canada, and Mexico.

3. The system was implemented with a strong emphasis on continuous improvement:

- A unique internal auditing/assessment approach was implemented that required quantifying cost savings that resulted from the project.

- A database was developed to track opportunities for cost savings that were identified in the project.

- Knowledge management tools were used in conjunction with the project to provide additional sources of information to help employees perform their jobs more effectively.

4. All processes were linked together with a hierarchical enterprise model that was combined with metrics to create a very well-integrated business management system. This included defined goals communicated throughout the company with accountability from top-level management to clerical levels. The system was used as a fundamental tool for developing new business management practices that resulted in:

- Higher levels of integration between field and corporate organizations

- Improved risk management in all business processes

- Much clearer understanding of how processes worked, formalized method for resolution of inconsistencies or improvement ideas within the processes, and a much clearer understanding of roles and responsibilities in the implementation and ongoing ownership of all processes

5. During the later part of this project, the company was involved in a very significant merger and the efforts to define standardized business processes helped lay the groundwork for new combined business processes to merge the efforts of the two companies.

Successfully implementing this effort required overcoming a number of difficult obstacles:

1. Senior Management Buy-in and Support

    - How to get senior management to actively support and actively become involved

    - How to continually justify the investment (time/money) to senior management

    - How to ensure the business system remains on senior management's goals and is cascaded down annually with metrics and true accountability

Solution:

    - Demonstrate the value to the business and make it clear and visible that the system is improving the business to internal as well as external customers.

    - Develop a quantifiable way to measure cost savings.

    - Integrate the program objectives into normal business objectives to make it part of the business management system.

    - Make senior management aware of the importance of their visible support.

2. Process Management

    - How to get "process owners" to own their processes, which includes "active" commitment to continual process optimization

    - How to maintain open-mindedness about new ideas and hard work to achieve "change" in a process

    - How to resolve process optimization implementation issues

Solution:

    - Strong and visible senior management support.

    - Address "What's in it for me?" from a process management perspective.

    - Create a process optimization approach where all participants feel it will be a "win/win" situation when completed.

- Provide an objective framework for analyzing and making decisions on process improvement approaches.

3. Employee Buy-in and Engagement

   - How to overcome employee skepticism (just another "program of the month").

   - How to gain full participation and commitment from all employees.

   - "Live the system" on an ongoing basis.

Solution:

- Strong and visible senior management support.

- Focus on achieving successes and communicate the word.

- Recognize employee achievements.

- Training, training, and more training.

ENDNOTES

1. ASQC Body of Knowledge, 1997.
2. D. A. Wren and R. G. Greenwood, *Management Innovators* (New York: Oxford University Press, 1998): 210–11.
3. M. Hammer and J. Champy, *Reengineering the Corporation: A Manifesto for Business Revolution* (New York: HarperBusiness, 1993).
4. M. Hammer, *Beyond Reengineering* (New York: HarperCollins, 1996): 81–83.
5. B. Sheehy, H. Bracey, and R. Frazier, *Winning the Race for Value* (New York: American Management Association, 1996): 112–14.
6. Rath and Strong Management Consultants, *Rath and Strong's Six Sigma Pocket Guide* (Lexington, MA: Rath & Strong Management Consultants, 2000).
7. G. Eckes, "Making Six Sigma Last (and Work)," *Ivey Business Journal* (January/February 2002): 77–81.
8. Ibid.
9. K. Ellis, "Mastering Six Sigma," *Training* (December 2001): 31–35.

7

The Role of Information Technology

CHAPTER OVERVIEW

Information technology is becoming very difficult, if not impossible, to separate from the business processes it is associated with. Integrating the design of business processes with the information systems that are associated with them is becoming increasingly important and is a major challenge for many companies.

New technology based on standards will allow companies to use modular, plug-and-play business objects and applications not only within the enterprise, but also across entire supply chains to support much more flexible and dynamic business processes. These new capabilities will further increase the challenge associated with designing and implementing integrated business processes and systems.

BACKGROUND

During the 1990s, American industry went on a spending binge for new technology. A recent study by Morgan Stanley indicated that companies wasted over $130 billion on technology spending over a two-year period ending in 2001.[1] In many cases, the problem is the same as it has been with other process improvement initiatives we have described—the IT effort was treated many times as a program in the same way that many other management "fads" were implemented. It was a single-dimensional solution to a much more complex multidimensional problem.

For example, companies might say, "We're going to do 'knowledge management' or we're going to do 'business intelligence'" in the same way they might say, "We're going to do 'TQM' or we're going to do 'Six

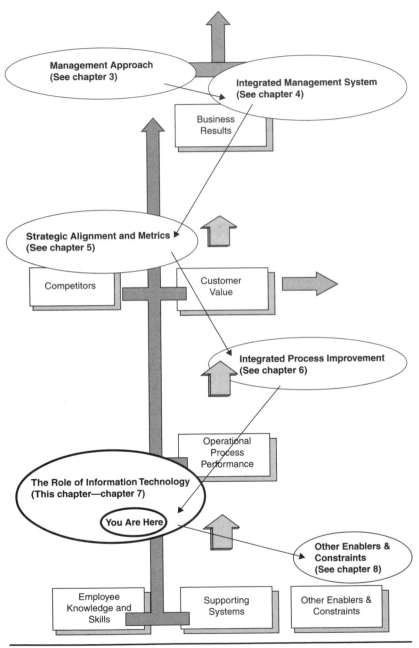

This navigational roadmap is intended to help readers understand the flow of information in these chapters and see how various topics fit into the overall model.

Sigma.'" That kind of effort sounds like a very neat thing to do; technology excites people and technology is often seen as a panacea to solving many different problems. However, unless that effort has some well-defined business goals that are directly tied to the company's business strategy and the technology component of the initiative is well integrated with any other related activities that might be part of a well-integrated process improvement project, it is not likely to be completely successful,

Good to Great by Jim Collins researched companies who made a transition from "good" to "great" and sustained being "great" for at least 15 years. They found that "technology by itself was never a primary root cause of either greatness or decline" and "Good to Great organizations avoid technology fads and bandwagons, yet they become pioneers in the application of carefully selected technology."[2]

The key thing is to understand the role information technology plays in the overall model:

- Information technology is both an enabler and a constraint. Innovative use of information technology can be a very powerful enabling force in the creation of significant business process improvements. On the other hand, inefficient and inflexible systems that are difficult to change can become a severe constraint.

- IT is an integral part of process designs. Because the implementation of information systems can be a gating item in many reengineering efforts, the design and development of information systems and the methodology associated with it needs to be an integral part of the business systems engineering discipline.

Information Technology as an Enabler

The role of information technology as an enabler is well understood. Davenport identifies nine different methods for using IT to enable process innovation, as shown in Table 7.1.[3]

From a very broad, long-term perspective, each major advance in IT has always been an enabler of new and more flexible organization structures. For example, distributed processing and client/server computing in the 1970s and 1980s were key factors that enabled breaking down large corporate bureaucracies. In today's world, the emergence of enterprise resource planning (ERP) systems and the evolution of new architectures based on standards with widespread internet and intranet connectivity will no doubt have an even more significant impact. The key point, however, is

Table 7.1   Roles of information technology.

Impact	Explanation
Automational	Eliminating human labor from a process (also reduces errors in tedious, repetitive tasks)
Informational	Capturing process information for purposes of understanding
Sequential	Changing process sequence or enabling parallelism
Tracking	Closely monitoring process status and objects
Analytical	Improving analysis of information and decision making
Geographical	Coordinating processes across distances
Integrative	Coordinating between tasks and processes
Disintermediating	Eliminating intermediaries from a process

Thomas H. Davenport, *Process Innovation* (Cambridge, MA: Harvard Business School Press, 1993): 51. Used by permission.

that technology needs to be implemented in the context of an overall business strategy to be successful.

Integrating Information Technology with Business Process Design

IT considerations should be a standard part of any business process improvement methodology such as Six Sigma; however, implementing a business process improvement initiative that contains a substantial component of information technology can be a very complex and risky project to manage and usually has significant cross-functional implications.

In many situations, the role of information technology is so integral to the process improvement effort that it cannot be separated. Appendix A provides an example of a simplified lifecycle model that can be used for managing this kind of effort. It provides a way for IT systems development efforts to be integrated with the business process design.

Some would argue that the design of the business process should precede the design and development of the IT systems that support it, as shown in Figure 7.1.

The argument for that approach is that the business and customer requirements should be the primary driving force behind process design and the process should not be constrained by an IT system approach. This approach might be ideal from that perspective; however, it has some very significant disadvantages:

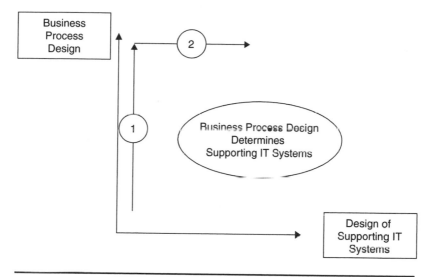

Figure 7.1 Customized IT system design approach.

- It can be very costly and extremely difficult to implement.

- It typically results in a large amount of custom software that would be difficult to support.

- It doesn't take advantage of off-the-shelf software to reduce development costs and risk.

This is exactly the approach that was popular prior to the advent of off-the-shelf ERP systems, and many very large, legacy COBOL systems that were nightmares to support resulted from this type of design approach.

The other extreme is shown in Figure 7.2. This approach was typically associated with ERP systems in the 1990s.

ERP systems typically come with the definition of the business processes "baked in" to the design of the system. The impact is that the system defines the business processes:

- Users are forced to adapt to the system.

- It minimizes the amount of custom software development.

- It restricts the flexibility of the system to adapt to unique requirements and changes.

Neither of these two approaches is ideal, and an integrated approach as shown in Figure 7.3 is probably much more optimized. A modern IT system can be an enabler of entirely different ways of doing things that might not

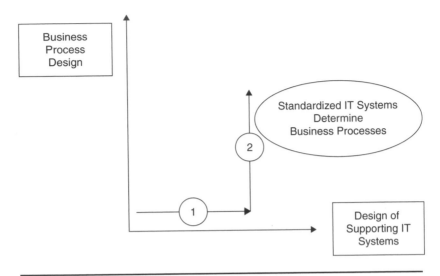

Figure 7.2   Standardized IT System Implementation.

be apparent if it is not considered as part of the design effort. That suggests a more synchronized approach, as shown in Figure 7.3.

Although that approach might be ideal, it has been very difficult to do because it would typically involve customizing the design of standard ERP systems to adapt them to business process requirements, and the design of ERP systems has not made that very practical. The alternatives have not been very attractive. The choices typically have been between:

- Highly customized systems similar to the old COBOL legacy systems that were popular prior to the introduction of ERP systems that can be extremely costly to develop and support

- Highly standardized ERP systems that are less expensive to develop and support, but can be somewhat inflexible because the definition of the business processes is typically "baked-in" to the system

Fortunately, new technology is emerging to provide a more practical alternative. New systems based on standards are rapidly evolving that will allow:

- More of a "plug-and-play" approach to mixing and matching a variety of applications as needed, instead of being locked in to a single large monolithic ERP system and the processes associated with it

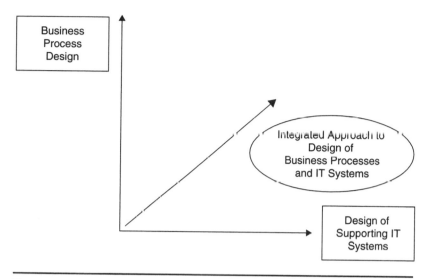

Figure 7.3 Integrated approach.

- Extraction of business processes from the design of systems and the use of standardized application interfaces to connect business process definition to the system implementation

See the section on "Standards-based Business Processes and Systems" for more details.

With this approach, businesses can use off-the-shelf packages for commodity processes that have little unique value for the business and selectively customize or develop other applications for processes that have more unique value to justify the cost of development and support. A standards-based, object-oriented approach would allow both the off-the-shelf applications process and the customized application process to coexist in a well-integrated environment. Figure 7.4 illustrates this approach.

ERP SYSTEMS AND THEIR IMPACT

In the 1990s, companies rapidly adopted ERP systems. ERP is an acronym for *Enterprise Resource Planning,* which is defined as "a business management system that integrates all facets of the business, including planning, manufacturing, sales, and marketing."[4] The goal of an ERP system is to tightly integrate the definition of the business processes and information systems and provide a common language and frame of reference for seamless exchange of information across the enterprise. Most ERP systems

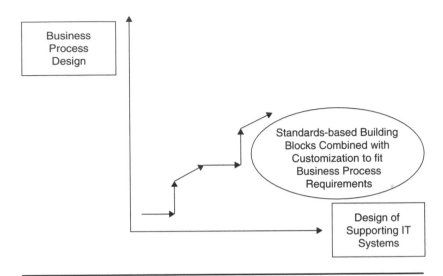

Figure 7.4   Building block approach.

include standard blueprints for common business processes. As a result, an ERP system:

•   Requires the adoption of a process orientation and promotes collaboration across the organization by developing a common understanding of how the process is defined, the information flows associated with it, and the roles and responsibilities of various functions for implementing and managing the process

•   Encourages the standardization of business processes across the organization and the use of proven best practices to reduce the cost and complexity of developing and maintaining the system

•   Standardizes information associated with the process and, as a result, makes it much easier to share and consolidate information:

> "ERP is a software mirror image of the major business processes of an organization, such as customer order fulfillment and manufacturing. Its success depends upon reach: A circumscribed ERP system isn't much better than the legacy system it replaces. In many cases, it is worse because the old code at least was written specifically for the company and the task. ERP's set of generic 'canned' processes shines only when used to connect parts of an organization. When a warehouse in Singapore enters a customer order, for example, that data flows automatically to others in the

company who need to see it—to the finance department at head-
quarters in New York and to the manufacturing department in
Europe."[5]

The Evolution of ERP Systems

The general evolution of ERP systems can be traced primarily to materials
requirements planning (MRP) systems that were originally created in the
1970s. MRP systems translated a master schedule for manufacturing of end
items into time-phased requirements for the subassemblies, components,
and raw materials planning and procurement.

> "In the 1980s, the concept of MRP-II (manufacturing resources
> planning) evolved, which was an extension of MRP to shop floor
> and distribution management activities. In the early 1990s, MRP-
> II was further extended to cover areas like engineering, finance,
> human resources, projects management, and so on—the complete
> gamut of activities within any business enterprise. Hence, the term
> ERP (Enterprise Resource Planning) was coined . . ."[6]

Risks and Rewards of ERP Systems

The value of implementing an ERP system can be high:

> "George Gilbert of DMG Technology Group in Menlo Park, CA
> . . . estimates that Fortune 1000 companies spend $50 billion a
> year on in-house programming. Buying something precrafted by
> SAP or its competitors can save a lot of money. And SAP's pack-
> aged software is likely to be more reliable and more up-to-date
> than anything a company could cobble together itself. A recent
> study by Deloitte & Touche found that when U.S. corporations
> replaced critical applications in 1996, 70 percent of the time they
> turned to packaged products."[7]

Implementation of large-scale ERP systems has very high risks: "It
crosses different organizations within a company. In addition, the investments are substantial in terms of buying the software and equipment, the
training required, and the amount of time spent. The scope and complexity
of reengineering all the company's business processes to fit with one of
these ERP systems is a very high-risk proposition":

> "It's an open secret that the ways to fail at ERP 'implementation'
> (one never simply installs ERP) outnumber the ways to succeed.

Horror stories range from technology glitches like Windows desktops that suddenly start speaking in German to heart-stopping charges—and, in the case of a company called Foxmeyer Drug, bankruptcy proceedings.

"The basic rap is that ERP systems are mind-bogglingly expensive and slow to install. Even a medium-sized installation can soak up tens of millions of dollars and require years of tweaking before benefits appear. Then there's the ERP support industry, an ecosystem of services and consultants whose bills can exceed the price of the software itself by a factor of 10."[8]

In spite of these risks, many companies have replaced aging legacy systems with ERP systems because a number of significant factors also have made them very attractive:

- Many existing legacy systems are expensive to operate and difficult to maintain and do not adapt well to modern client/server computing architectures.

- They are also very difficult to modify and adapt to changing market requirements and more distributed organization structures.

- ERP systems eliminated any year 2000 problems that may have been present in existing legacy applications, and they also comply with the new requirements of the European Economic and Monetary Union by mid-2002.

- The benefits of replacing legacy systems with modern technology are significant, but the primary advantage of an ERP system is in the area of improved business processes:

"The most important thing to remember is that the real problems with ERP systems like those made by SAP come pretty much from the same place as the benefits—that is, from reengineering a company's core business processes to take advantage of the software. 'It's a huge mistake to think about ERP as a technology initiative instead of a business project,' says Bruce Richardson, VP for research strategy at AMR. 'About 80 percent of the benefits come from what you change in your business. The software is just an enabler.'"[9]

- ERP systems also provide a well-integrated environment with a consistent data model that makes it much easier to share information across the whole company.

Overall Impact of ERP Systems

ERP systems are an example of a situation in which the technology has advanced faster than our ability to manage it. Successful design and implementation of ERP systems force several things to happen which will accelerate the development of a new approach to management:

1. Systems Thinking

    To some extent, ERP systems encourage systems thinking because they are process oriented and help integrate a number of functions in the company around a common definition of company business processes.

2. Planning and Management

    The integration of business processes and associated information systems requires companies to more fully integrate the management of those efforts. The typical functional organization structure found in most companies today does not lend itself to doing that easily and it requires people with a broad cross-functional perspective to do it effectively.

    "It is important to recognize that this is a business-driven initiative, not an information-systems initiative, and you have to have extensive user involvement," emphasizes Martin. "The processes and the businesses were reengineered before we started the SAP project, so that wasn't an afterthought. The model developed was to reflect how we wanted to conduct our business, not what was possible through the availability of some given piece of software. Other companies that have proceeded without that overall business model have found a year or 18 months later that they had to back up the truck and [have] some coordination and fundamental structure that could be used across business units."[10]

3. Disciplined and Integrated Methodology

    ERP systems have forced companies to adopt a much more disciplined and integrated methodology for managing the implementation as well as the planning of the system, and the implementation of a large-scale ERP system is a gut-wrenching experience for most companies. Robert S. Putrus has identified eight major reasons why ERP projects will not succeed:[11]

    a. There is no executive sponsor. Putrus points out that ERP crosses functions within a company. Therefore, the program needs someone with the authority to bring various functional managers together.

b. The project is viewed as being just of interest to finance. Or information systems (IS). Or manufacturing . . . It is all, not one.

c. There is no full-time project manager.

d. Because of the hardware/software communications intensity, the IS people make the decisions. The problem here, Putrus points out, is that they may not have a good understanding of the functional requirements.

e. No one does due diligence on the vendor.

f. There is no documentation of the implementation procedure.

g. Reengineering of processes is essential, Putrus suggests, if the effort is made to implement ERP of existing processes.

h. There is a massive change of everything.

4. Process Management Focus and Process Discipline

Implementation of broad-scale ERP systems force companies to focus on business processes and reach agreement on how the processes work across all the organizations that may be involved. The benefits of achieving that can be significant, but it is typically difficult to achieve because many companies do not operate that way today. Process discipline does not necessarily mean that processes are rigidly followed in all cases; but, at a minimum, it implies that the company is aware of what its major processes are and how they work, and makes conscious decisions about how they are designed and implemented.

"In medieval times, cathedrals were usually built without any real blueprints. The master builder had a vague idea of what he wanted to do and then he began to build. As he went along, the patron might want some changes made, some structures might fail, or the builder himself might want to work on new styles from Italy or France. Rather than start anew, the builder would incorporate any modifications, and, using his experience, he'd keep working until something resembling a cathedral was completed. Usually the initial design looked nothing like the end product. Sometimes it worked out (those buildings still stand today); sometimes it didn't (the roof caved in on an unsuspecting congregation)."[12]

There is a legitimate question of how much flexibility companies need to give up while adopting the process discipline that may be required by an ERP system. New approaches are evolving based on standards that make it possible to gain many of the process discipline advantages of an ERP system without being locked in to a single, large monolithic system.

5.　Customer Value Perspective

Some very significant strategic decisions and tradeoffs are needed in developing an ERP strategy. It requires deciding which systems and processes really contribute a unique competitive advantage to the value proposition that is critical to the company's success and should not be standardized versus others that add little unique value and stand a lot to gain from standardization to reduce costs and complexity.

"Any company has to view ERP within the context of its overall business. Tom Davenport argues that as ERP becomes ubiquitous, senior execs should consider a new set of questions. What are the real business processes that bring us our identity and our competitive advantage? How can we be sure that we really have some unique capability there? Compaq Computer, for example, maintains its edge by keeping ERP software out of areas like product forecasting."[13]

It is becoming impossible to view the implementation of these systems as an IT initiative. This will put even more pressure on organizations to adapt to this new technology. Effective implementation will only come from developing a methodology to integrate the IT role into the overall design and development of business process improvement initiatives.

The obstacles to achieving effective integration of the IT function are generally as much organizational as they are technological. Some form of cross-functional management is needed with a sufficiently broad perspective of process management, process improvement, and information technology disciplines to create more effective and balanced strategies and plans.

The downside of most ERP systems is that the definition of the business process is typically "baked in" to the design of the ERP system. The ability to customize the design and processes associated with these systems is typically very limited, and extensive customization can lead to significant support issues. As a result, the technology associated with ERP systems has typically forced companies to accept whatever processes came with the system, and few companies have really undertaken an integrated approach to designing processes and the information systems associated with the process.

ERP Systems and Supply Chains

In today's world, traditional sequential supply chains are collapsing and becoming much more complex:

- Information technology plays a critical role in facilitating these supply chains that require much higher levels of information sharing to operate effectively.

- New standards-based systems that make it easier to share information across enterprise boundaries will accelerate these changes significantly.

Supply chains significantly complicate the business problem to be solved. ERP systems were primarily oriented to integrate applications, processes, and data *within an enterprise*; they have limited ability to integrate an entire supply chain that might include different companies with different kinds of ERP systems, different types of databases, and so on. The only way to do that level of integration is either:

- Force all companies in the supply chain to use the same kind of ERP system (not likely to happen).

- Develop standards that would allow different kinds of ERP systems to be able to interact with each other and share data. This is exactly what the next generation of standards-based systems is all about.

The implementation of ERP systems in the 1990s has been very significant and has had a big impact on integrating business processes with the systems associated with implementing them within an enterprise. In today's world, however, there are even greater changes just beginning to evolve that will have an even greater impact.

STANDARDS-BASED BUSINESS PROCESSES AND SYSTEMS

New information architectures are rapidly evolving based on industry standards that will dramatically redefine and expand how computing is done over the Internet. These architectures will integrate entire supply chains all the way from the consumer to the ultimate producer of the product or service.

What is emerging is a huge, new information infrastructure consisting of information building blocks (business objects) that are put together like

"Lego" blocks to create seamless and secure information architectures that transparently connect consumers directly to products and services through a variety of intermediate applications and companies. Like "Lego" blocks, these information systems building blocks can be rapidly and dynamically disassembled and reassembled in different ways, as business needs change. There will be at least four different levels of "Lego" blocks that compose this broad architecture:

- *Inter-Enterprise:* Companies will begin to expose standard interfaces through Web services that can be accessed directly by other applications in other companies.

- *Application Integration:* Applications will expose standard interfaces to processes. Documents and data used by those applications will also become standardized to allow them to be easily integrated into an overall business process.

- *Custom Application Development:* There will be a much stronger emphasis on object-oriented building blocks to create modular software components, which encourage reusability and rapid application development.

- *Consumer:* The combination of authentication, billing services, and Web services will replace the consumer's PC with an Internet appliance.

What enables this architecture to have such widespread impact is that it is designed around interfaces built on industry standards. If the "Lego" blocks come in a variety of shapes and sizes with different interconnect mechanisms, it will be impossible to achieve this vision of an interconnected applications, systems, and enterprises. If information applications are created one-at-a-time by skilled craftsmen without interchangeable parts, the infrastructure will be difficult or impossible to maintain. Only a much higher level of emphasis on standards can ensure a stable infrastructure upon which business processes and systems functionality can rely.

The significant impact, however, is that this infrastructure allows business process designers to design a business process and then connect application components into that process to implement it. Microsoft ".Net" is an example of a standards-based architecture and is discussed in more detail in additional reading in Appendix B. Using this architecture:

- The definition of the process is done in the "Orchestration Designer," which is a Visio interface for both Commerce Server and Biztalk Server.

- Modular components are used to implement the process to allow the definition of the process to be more flexible (the Visio process definition connects the modular components that implement the process with the process flow).

- Application integration components are used to integrate a variety of applications into the process.

Implementation of these capabilities will force the cross-functional coupling of business process design and systems implementation to merge even closer than they have during the implementation of ERP systems in the 1990s. It is no longer feasible to treat the design of business processes as a separate activity from the design and implementation of the systems associated with implementing those processes.

With ERP systems, the design of the business process may have been dictated largely by the system that implemented it; the challenge today is that we are perhaps finally at a point that the design of the business process can drive the design of the systems that support it, which is the way it should have been all along. Many companies had a difficult time implementing ERP systems and this presents an even greater challenge that might go well beyond that. The tradeoff may be to continue to accept "canned" business processes and systems or invest in resources to design and implement customized business processes and systems only where it will provide competitive advantage.

The ability to integrate business processes across the entire supply chain will also open up huge opportunities to dramatically change the way companies do business over the Internet and potentially even collapse some existing supply chains. Taking advantage of the capabilities this new technology enables could drive a very large reengineering effort to fully realize their impact. These trends will also put increased pressure on accelerating the need for the discipline of "business systems engineering."

Business Needs

The major challenges businesses face in today's environment that a standards-based architecture will address can be broken down into three areas:

1. Inter-Enterprise Communications

   The advents of supply chains and complex business relationships that are typical today have created an urgent need to share information of many kinds across enterprise boundaries:

- If I am a supplier to Wal-Mart, how do I effectively share information with them to jointly maximize the effectiveness of our supply chain?

- What if we have different kinds of ERP systems? How do I get the two systems to talk to each other and share data?

Electronic document interchange (EDI) provides a method to connect two independent business systems that have a limited requirement for sharing information based on well-defined transactions. What is needed in many cases is more tightly connected business systems, where the business processes in one company are essentially an extension of the business processes in the other. EDI trading partner relationships can also be time consuming to setup and often somewhat inflexible.

2. Application Integration

Within an enterprise, companies typically have a mixture of different applications that do not necessarily share information effectively. Enterprise resource planning (ERP) systems have helped solve this problem, but that approach typically creates another whole set of problems:

- Implementing a large, monolithic ERP system like SAP provides a consistent application framework for the entire company and provides for consistency of data across the enterprise, but it makes it difficult to use other applications that might be more optimal for an individual function within the company.

- It also typically forces the company to give up their own business processes and to adopt whatever processes are hard-coded into the ERP system. These "baked-in" processes are difficult to customize to fit unique requirements.

The overall challenge is: How do you create an environment that is architecturally consistent to facilitate sharing of documents and data and retain the flexibility to use different applications as necessary and customize or dynamically change the business processes as needed to meet new requirements?

3. Technology Integration

At a technology level, there are significant challenges:

- What languages and operating systems should be used to develop customized application solutions? There are many choices available among languages and operating systems. Whatever choice you pick has tended to lock you into that technology, a technology that may be incompatible with other alternative application technologies.

- How do we keep customized application development activities well aligned with the business process requirements they are intended to support? Many companies have developed large, customized applications that are difficult to maintain and support, may not be aligned with the associated processes, and are difficult to adapt to changes in business requirements.

How can we quickly develop customized business applications to meet rapidly changing requirements? How can we stay within a very constrained budget for development and support? How can we avoid a situation where the way the business operates is defined by the systems and the technology used to implement the business systems? Some legacy COBOL systems exemplify these problems.

Vision for the Future

The computing vision of the future encapsulates the entire Internet as a very powerful and tightly interconnected infrastructure to support new ways of doing business. The vision is one in which the end-consumer or buyer is tightly connected through whatever intermediate suppliers are involved to the ultimate producer of the product or service. This is accomplished through powerful and dynamic real-time connections. Microsoft calls this "One Degree of Separation." As an example, consider the following: If a man wants to buy a shirt today, he goes into a department store, shops through the various styles and sizes, and picks out a shirt in his approximate size. That shirt arrived at the store through some kind of distribution network with probably at least one layer of intermediate distributor, the shirt manufacturer, and the retail store.

Some years ago, it was popular to order custom-made shirts from the Far East where a shirt could be made to your exact measurements, including a monogram if desired. It was an awkward process to send your exact measurements to the Far East and it could easily take a month or two to make the shirts and have them delivered. These shirts were somewhat expensive because they were tailored by hand to the customer's exact measurements. There was also a high probability for error. You typically got exactly what you ordered even if the order had an error in it.

Imagine that, instead of going into a retail store to buy a shirt in a standard size off the shelf that might "approximately" fit, your exact measurements are stored in an XML data format that can be transmitted to the ultimate shirt manufacturer. And imagine the possibility that instead of shopping for a shirt through retail outlets or pointing and clicking through Web sites to find a shirt supplier, that there was an online personal clothing agent that did that for you. The "clothing agent" would know your style preferences and your exact measurements and could transmit your order for a shirt directly to the assembly line, where it is produced and shipped the next day.

Impact of Standards-Based Systems

This is a very powerful new capability, but it is a double-edged sword. It offers businesses huge new capabilities that have never been available before, but on the other hand, it requires a level of sophistication to fully take advantage of these capabilities that most businesses are not well prepared for. Refer to Table 7.2.

KNOWLEDGE MANAGEMENT AND QUALITY SYSTEMS

The concept of *knowledge management* has been getting a lot of attention in many areas of industry, and it raises questions about how it affects existing efforts to define and implement quality systems (based on ISO 9000 or other standards).

- Is knowledge management just another fad?

- How are knowledge management and quality systems related?

This chapter discusses some of the fundamental trends that are behind the convergence of these technology areas and a framework for understanding how they complement each other to create highly empowered and dynamic business systems for the 21st century.

What is Knowledge Management?

Knowledge management is an evolving technology area and it is very difficult to find a standard definition of what it is. Here are two possible definitions:

"Knowledge management is the strategy and processes to enable the creation and flow of relevant knowledge throughout the business to

Table 7.2 Impact of standards-based systems.

Capability	Implication
Define modular and dynamic information systems based on "plug-and-play" applications architecture that are designed to support business processes	• Business process designers will be able to take a much more integrated approach to the design of business processes and the information systems associated with them, rather than being limited to "off-the-shelf" monolithic ERP systems that come with the processes "baked in" to them. • The level of complexity of this design effort just increased dramatically and will force companies to take a more integrated approach to how they design business processes and information systems.
Standards will allow businesses to much more freely and easily exchange information and data of all kinds	• This opens the door to much tighter integration of the supply chain, all the way from the consumer to the ultimate supplier of the material. • It potentially offers the opportunity for a significant amount of reengineering to take advantage of this new technology that might collapse entire supply chains and offer huge productivity gains. • This also significantly expands the complexity of defining integrated business processes and systems because it now extends well beyond the traditional enterprise boundaries.
Collapsing of supply chains (mentioned above) could provide much more direct access by consumers to suppliers (and by suppliers to ultimate consumers)	• This could change the "playing field" significantly. The manufacturers who are the ultimate producer of goods currently may be somewhat isolated from the direct consumer. This new technology potentially offers the capability to break down some of those barriers between the manufacturer and the ultimate consumer. • Manufacturers who are prepared to take advantage of that might have an opportunity to gain significant strategic advantage, but it also requires a level of complexity that they may not be used to dealing with.

create organizational, customer, and consumer value." David Smith, Unilever[14]

"Knowledge management is the broad process of locating, organizing, transferring, and using the information and expertise within an organization. The overall knowledge management process is supported by four key enablers: leadership, culture, technology, and measurement." American Productivity and Quality Center[15]

Although many of the essential elements of knowledge management are not new, the integration of those elements into an overall strategy for effectively managing knowledge to achieve strategic business advantage is still an evolving science.

> "Learning organizations are skilled at five main activities: systematic problem solving, experimentation with new approaches, learning from their own experience and past history, learning from the experiences and best practices of others, and transferring knowledge quickly and efficiently throughout the organization. Each is accompanied by a distinctive mindset, tool kit, and pattern of behavior. Many companies practice these activities to some degree. But few are consistently successful because they rely on happenstance and isolated examples. By creating systems and processes that support these activities and integrating them into the fabric of daily operations, companies can manage their learning more effectively." [16]

There are a number of questions that an effective knowledge management strategy should address:

- What types of knowledge are critical to the company's business?

- How does that knowledge impact the company's business performance?

- Where and how is that knowledge managed in today's environment?

- What could be done to better utilize that knowledge to gain competitive advantage?

Four types of Knowledge Management projects have been identified in a recent article in the *Sloan Management Review*:[17]

1. Create Knowledge Repositories

2. Improve Knowledge Access

3. Enhance Knowledge Environment

4. Manage Knowledge as an Asset

Successful implementation of all of these techniques involves recognition of the importance of *knowledge* as an enabler of business excellence and requires developing an understanding of how it can be used to develop competitive advantage. Knowledge management, in itself, is not an overall solution to any business problem; however, each of these different approaches may be appropriate to some degree as part of a high performance business system. Effectively planning the design of business systems requires using knowledge management as a tool in the appropriate context to maximize the goals of the business.

Knowledge management, if it is applied correctly, is not another fad— in fact, very little of the technology is radically new, but it is very likely to become the most important factor in many businesses to determine competitive success. The need to more effectively manage knowledge has become more urgent due to the rapid expansion of information and the broad proliferation of computers and worldwide communications capabilities, such as the Internet. Companies that ignore those trends are likely to lose competitive advantage while the payoff from increased focus on knowledge management can be significant in a number of areas:

1. Product Development and Innovation

   Probably the highest impact area is in the development of new products and services. O'Dell and Grayson identify two major potential areas of benefit in that area:[18]

   • Getting the Right Product Out

   More effectively using market and customer information to help guide the development of products and services can substantially reduce the risk of new product development. Hewlett Packard, for example, maintains a large database of customer comments about products called the "Voice of the Customer." When an HP employee receives a customer complaint, comment, or suggestion for improvement of any kind about an HP product or service, he/she can input it into their database. The development engineers and product managers can use that information to help plan future products.

   • Getting Products Out the Right Way

   "Companies that have experience with the development of new products should know what works and what doesn't. Yet, more often than not, the experience and learning of past development efforts do not make their way in an organized and deliberate fashion to current initiatives. The result is costly waste of time and resources ... To eliminate unnecessary delays, companies can bring together people who've been through the new product development process with those who are developing the next generation, in order to: (1) avoid prior mistakes, (2) build on market knowledge, and (3) cut cycle time."[19]

Boeing is noted for very successfully applying the use of past lessons learned to design the new 777 aircraft, which has been recognized as probably the most successful design effort in the company's history. Chrysler also uses this technique in their "Books of Knowledge" to capture lessons learned from prior automotive design efforts.

2.   Operational Effectiveness and Employee Productivity

Using knowledge effectively to leverage employee productivity and operational effectiveness can also have a very large impact. A prime example would be sharing information regarding best practices to improve operational performance. Other examples would be using information more effectively in knowledge-intensive areas of the business, such as using knowledge bases to rapidly identify and implement solutions in the customer service area.

3.   Customer Intimacy

Finally, more effectively organizing and tracking what is known about particular customer needs and preferences can help a business customize its products and services to particular customers. This is a key goal that customer relationship management (CRM) systems are intended to accomplish.

Knowledge management and information management are not the same thing. *Information management* typically is focused on data; knowledge is data put into a context that has meaning and includes other forms of "information" that typically would not be found in an information system, such as tacit knowledge that exists in the minds of employees in the company. The "people" dimension of knowledge management is very important and naturally includes learning and growth initiatives and cultural initiatives to promote sharing of information.

Knowledge management is more of a way of thinking about how to manage a company in terms of its knowledge as a strategic asset. The assumption behind it is that the value of the company is based on its knowledge and knowledge needs to be viewed and developed as a strategic asset. Information management provides the "infrastructure" to support knowledge management. Without information management, knowledge management would be impossible; but information management, in itself, does not go far enough. What has really fueled the interest in knowledge management is the Internet and corporate intranets. There is such a huge amount of raw data and information out there that it is overwhelming . . . there needs to be some intelligent way to make some sense out of it. Knowledge management provides that higher-level context.

Relationship of Knowledge Management & Quality

As quality systems take on a broader role, it is much easier to see the relationship to knowledge management. To see that relationship, it is essential to view the quality system not in the traditional "quality control" perspective, but in a broader perspective that emphasizes empowerment and enablement as well as control.

Knowledge management is a key technology to use in building quality systems designed for continuous improvement:

- It empowers employees with information at their fingertips to do their jobs more effectively.

- It provides a "knowledge repository" for lessons learned and other information that is essential to continuous improvement.

Knowledge management is beginning to make the transition from an intellectual area of study to a more pragmatic approach that can be implemented in actual practice to drive business results. It is becoming recognized that an effective knowledge management system must be based on:

- A way of capturing and organizing explicit as well as tacit knowledge of how the business operates, including an understanding of how current business processes function

- A "systems-approach" to management that facilitates assimilation of new knowledge into the business system and is oriented toward continuous improvement/innovation

- A common framework for managing knowledge and some way of validating and synthesizing new knowledge as it is acquired

- A culture and values that support collaborative sharing of knowledge across functions and encourage full participation of all employees in the process

Without those basic elements as a foundation, it is unlikely that any knowledge management effort would succeed. Those are, in fact, the same elements that are at the heart of an effective quality system:

- The idea of explicitly defining how a business operates and the processes associated with it is one of the most fundamental requirements of quality systems, such as ISO 9000.

- An underlying principle of ISO 9000 is the emphasis on the overall management system. Quality is based not just on having effective process controls, but on having an effective overall management system that provides a framework for continuous improvement.

- The document and data control requirements of ISO 9000 require companies to define a process for ensuring that any critical information that is required for the performance of a business process is accurate, up-to-date, and effective for its intended purpose.

- Because ISO 9000 places an emphasis on processes that in many cases are cross-functional in nature, it forces companies to break down some of the organizational and functional "stovepipes" that inhibit effective sharing of information.

EXAMPLES OF LEVERAGING QUALITY AND BUSINESS RESULTS

Knowledge management, like quality, has to be defined in the context of the business it serves and, in fact, it can take on very different meanings in different organizations that have different goals of what they want to achieve with it. Both should be aligned with driving business results and that requires an understanding of the cause-and-effect relationships and how the business operates as a system. A good strategy should answer the following questions:

- What is the business strategy? Who are the customers? What are their needs and expectations? Who are the competitors? How does the business seek to differentiate itself to gain competitive advantage?

- What are the customer values that have the most important impact on business results and what are the internal factors that have the greatest impact on maximizing customer value?

- What role does "knowledge" play in achieving those results? What kind of quality system approach is appropriate?

Tables 7.3 through 7.5 show a few examples of how quality systems and knowledge management efforts might be organized to support improving customer value in each of these areas.

Operational Excellence

Table 7.3 Operational excellence knowledge management applications.

Customer Value	Quality System Strategy	Knowledge Management Approach
• Maximize efficiency and effectiveness of internal processes to reduce costs • Improve reliability and consistency of products and services	• Well-defined processes, standardization, and good process control • Strong emphasis on continuous process improvement • Cross-functional teams to optimize overall process performance	• Detailed knowledge of processes and performance • Sharing of best practices across the organization and benchmarking with other companies

Examples:

1. **"Chevron** CEO Ken Derr boasted of reducing operating costs by $2 billion over the last seven years. He gave KM credit. 'Of all the initiatives we've undertaken, few have been as important or rewarding as our efforts to build a learning organization by sharing and managing knowledge throughout our company,' he said."[20]

2. **UnumProvident** has implemented a new portal that will provide 11,000 employees with a unified process for enterprise information access and decision making to support ongoing business operations, to increase customer service and satisfaction, and to improve employee communications and faster time to market by integrating multiple intranets and providing personalized, role-based views of enterprise information and selected external sources.

   "'Our overarching vision is to have a single point of entry to the company's full range of resources,' explains J. Harold Chandler, chairman, president, and CEO of UnumProvident. 'In addition, the portal will provide a means for capturing and sharing best practices—in short, improving our *corporate IQ*.'"

   ". . . According to company CIO Robert O. Best, 'If employees can access pertinent information easily, they will be able to make critical business decisions quickly and with confidence, whether that employee is in a call center or in the board room. Ultimately, this will reduce cost, increase customer satisfaction levels, improve the quality of decisions, and decrease our sales cycle time.'"

3. **"Hallmark Cards** installed Demand Solution from Yantra to manage customer orders and inventory across various channels, online retailers, internal business units, third-party suppliers, and service providers.

   "The benefits of the software for Hallmark have included a reduction in the time and costs involved in coordinating and fulfilling orders, according to a recent press release from Yantra. It also extends Hallmark's existing enterprise resource planning (ERP) infrastructure, and is said to give Hallmark.com the flexibility and scalability to add new third-party product offerings and services, and to integrate with other distribution channels."[21]

Product Leadership

Table 7.4   Product leadership knowledge management applications.

Customer Value	Quality System Strategy	Knowledge Management Approach
• Improve time-to-market for new product development • Develop leadership products and services to capture maximum market share	• Proven and reliable methods for developing products and services • Effectively managing the risks of product development efforts • Collaboration among all functions to improve time-to-market	• Capturing of "lessons learned" from previous projects • Knowledge sharing among functions and with customers and suppliers

Examples:

1. **Daimler Chrysler** has deployed "Books of Knowledge" throughout the company to capture product design information so that lessons learned from past design efforts will be preserved.

2. **Lockheed Martin** has implemented 'LiveLink' document management and sharing software to "collect design information for developing manufacturing concepts for the new Joint Strike Fighter aircraft from suppliers and partners around the world."[22]

3. **Rhone-Poulenc Rorer** (Collegeville, PA) is "pointing to Documentum's (www.documentum.com) EDMS 98 as part of the reason for speeding the regulatory approval for 18 drugs. This enables us to get new drugs to patients who need them as quickly as possible. And on the bottom line, considering that some individual drugs generate revenues of a million dollars a day, such time-savings can translate into huge profits."[23]

4. **J.D. Edwards,** with 6000 employees in 50 offices worldwide, "to answer the demands of competitive pressure and to ensure that all employees have access to comprehensive product and market information, the software developer focused its talents inward. The result was an enterprisewide intranet-based employee communication tool, the 'Knowledge Garden' . . . On average, 95 percent of employees use the Knowledge Garden for approximately 10 minutes each day . . . The most tangible result is immediate access to standardized operating information, which has meant that the 14-month sales cycle of the pre-Knowledge Garden era has been cut nearly in half, and is now at eight months."[24]

5. **The National Institute on Drug Abuse (NIDA),** which is part of the National Institutes of Health, has developed a Web-based Clinical Trials Network to foster greater collaboration and more effective communication in conducting its mission. To support its mission of enlisting science to fight drug abuse and addiction, NIDA has established the Clinical Trials Network to develop and deliver new treatment options to patients in community clinical settings.

Customer Intimacy

Table 7.5   Customer intimacy knowledge management applications.

Customer Value	Quality System Strategy	Knowledge Management Approach
• Emphasis on customer service as a driver of business performance • Products and services customized as needed to fit particular customer needs	• Empowerment of frontline employees to resolve problems and satisfy customers • Effective and responsive management of customer satisfaction	• Use knowledge of unique customer needs and requirements to customize products and services as needed • Improved problem-solving capabilities

Examples

1. **BankBoston** has implemented an Electronic Document Warehouse to give approximately 5000 internal online users the ability to access information from more than 15 million pages of documents. "We are continually looking at ways to improve responsiveness to our customers," said Edwin Kane, senior group manager of information delivery services at BankBoston. "Being able to retrieve and quickly view documents and information will enable us to both better serve customers and improve our organizational efficiency."[26]

2. **Shared Medical Alternatives** (Riverside, CA) is enhancing its customer service by reducing the turnaround time for claim reimbursements. "By implementing TeleForm with Medisys, a document claim or billing form can go from being received to adjudication to claims processing all in the same afternoon, without human intervention," said Mark Oja, president of Medisys Technologies. "TeleForm also works with our proprietary archive and retrieval solution, which will enable our customer service department to have immediate access to an image of a submitted claim form when responding to inquiries made by doctors and clients."[27]

3. **TaylorMade-Adidas Golf**, a well-known golf equipment manufacturer, implemented a Web-based contact center solution to ensure that its customer service was equal to the task of responding to highly technical equipment questions from both consumers and retailers.

   ". . . The software already is said to have helped the manufacturer gain a better understanding of consumer issues, improve response times, reduce staffing, and create a conduit for dialogue with its consumers, according to a recent press release from KANA.

   ". . . The new Response software, according to the release, reduces training time and ensures the consistent quality of consumer service responses. An automated solution suggestion system provides reps with a database of answers to common consumer inquiries, and those responses are instantly accessible via hot keys. The new system also enables the reps to funnel highly technical questions to product engineering and marketing experts, ensuring their timely response and allowing managers to monitor each rep's work.

Continued

Table 7.5	*Continued*

... 'As a result of the implementation,' McClellan says, 'TaylorMade-Adidas Golf now provides faster and higher-quality consumer service with one-third fewer resources. We also have a more productive connection with our consumers, providing us with a better view of what's happening in the marketplace and empowering us with information that we can pass on to our internal teams for immediate action.'[28]

A well-designed quality system and a knowledge management approach are almost inseparable and each supports the other. Both have common goals of creating an environment that supports learning and continuous improvement.

However, both quality systems and knowledge management are *tools* to help achieve business goals. Many companies have fallen into the trap of pursuing the latest management "fad" rather than keeping the primary focus on defining the goals to achieve in the business system, and *then as a second step*, examine how both quality systems and knowledge management help achieve those goals.

A very simple example is shown in Figure 7.5. Some businesses, by their very nature, require high levels of control and consistency and have less need for innovation. Some are at the other extreme and have higher knowledge content and a greater need for ongoing innovation.

The optimum point would probably be at different points on this spectrum for different types of businesses. A nuclear power plant, for example, has a need for a very high level of control and consistency, and any "innovation" must be carefully controlled because of the associated risks and issues.

Having a defined system for managing quality and process improvement should be a foundation for almost any knowledge management system to be effective, and both efforts can be very complementary if they are used as tools to achieve a company's business objectives. The key to that synergy is a well-designed business management system that provides an overall framework for both. The full benefits of either approach will not be realized unless they are aligned with achieving business results and implemented as part of an overall systems approach to management.

The implementation of such a fully integrated business system that provides all the benefits of a modern quality system as well as knowledge management capabilities can be quite complex and requires a considerable amount of planning and skill to implement effectively. It is a multidimensional problem and involves a broad level of cross-functional collaboration that many companies are not well organized to support; however, there are immediate opportunities for companies that recognize the interrelationship of these two technology areas:

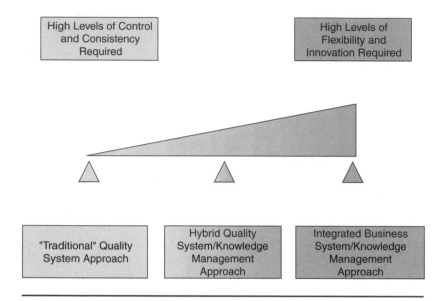

Figure 7.5   Relationship between control and flexibility.

1. Companies that have implemented systems for managing quality can revitalize those systems and make them more dynamic and more effective by incorporating knowledge management capabilities.

2. Companies that are considering knowledge management efforts can improve the probability of success and effectiveness of those efforts by understanding the benefit to be gained by having a well-designed business and quality management system as a foundation.

In either case, the approach should be focused on achieving real and measurable business results and should be designed for incremental growth so that it can easily evolve as the technology in this area evolves.

ENDNOTES

1. J. Hopkins and M. Kessler, "Companies Squander Billions on Tech," *USA Today* (20 May 2002): 1.
2. J. Collins, *Good to Great* (HarperCollins, 2001): 162.
3. T. H. Davenport, *Process Innovation* (Cambridge, MA: Harvard Business School Press, 1993): 51.
4. "ERP Definition," www.pcwebopedia.com/ERP.htm.
5. "ERP Supply Chain Research Center," www.cio.com/forums/erp/.

6. "ERP—Software Strategies," www.microsoft.com/industry/entapp/features/4microsoft.htm.
7. D. Kilpatrick et al., "10 Tech Trends to Bet On," *Fortune* (November 10, 1997): 102.
8. M. H. Martin, "An ERP Strategy," *Fortune* (February 2, 1998).
9. Ibid.
10. T. Stevens, "Kodak Focuses on ERP," *Industry Week* (August 18, 1997).
11. G. S. Vasilash, "How To—and How Not To—Implement ERP," *Automotive Manufacturing and Production* (August 1997).
12. T. Curran and G. Keller, *SAP R/3 Business Blueprint* (Englewood Cliffs, NJ: Prentice Hall, 1998): 22.
13. See note 8.
14. "Quotes on Knowledge Management," wbln0018.worldbank.org/HRS/yournet.nsf/yournet/DynaFrame?OpenDocument&Page=7FC464245c5B04208525687E00.
15. Ibid.
16. D. A. Garvin, "Building a Learning Organization," *Harvard Business Review on Knowledge Management* (1998): 52.
17. Davenport, et al., "How Can Organizations Use Knowledge More Effectively?" *Sloan Management Review* (winter 1998): 44–57.
18. C. O'Dell and C. J. Jackson Jr., *If Only We Knew What We Know* (New York: Free Press, 1998): 50–51.
19. Ibid.
20. "KM in Practice: Improving corporate IQ," *KMWorld* (January 1, 2002).
21. "KM in Practice: When you care to e-send the very best," *KMWorld* (January 1, 2002).
22. "Fighter program gets collaborative tool," *KMWorld* (March 1, 1999).
23. "Rhone-Poulenc Rorer speeds drug regulatory submissions," *KMWorld* (April 1, 1999).
24. "Competition fosters innovation," *KMWorld* (June 1, 1999).
25. "KM in Practice: Clinical trial collaboraiton," *KMWorld* (March 1, 2002).
26. "BankBoston delivers better access," *KMWorld* (April 1, 1999).
27. "Cardiff Software Announces Contract with Shared Medical Alternatives," www.cardiff.com/PressRelease/P1054/P1054.htm.
28. "KM in Practice: IT to a tee," *KMWorld* (January 1, 2002).

8

Other Enablers and Constraints

CHAPTER OVERVIEW

Developing an effective and well-integrated process improvement approach is more than just a methodology, it is also critical to create an environment that is conducive to the implementation of that methodology. Some built-in constraints must be overcome in most organizations to do that.

A system designed for continuous improvement must especially be aware of the obstacles that must be overcome to implement change. The most difficult problem in implementing TQM and reengineering efforts is overcoming some of the constraints that are inherent in all organizations. Constraints generally act to maintain the status quo and resist efforts to change.

There are several categories of constraints that affect process improvement and change efforts:

- Cultural and Behavioral Factors

- Organizational Structure

- Technology

These factors influence both incremental and more radical improvement efforts; however, the level of the resistance is generally proportional to the magnitude and impact of the change. Many improvement initiatives flounder because they fail to take into consideration the constraints that will limit successful implementation or they attempt to overcome the constraints with a "brute force" approach. Identification of constraints, evaluation of their risk, and planning appropriate intervention methods is an essential part of any process change or improvement initiative.

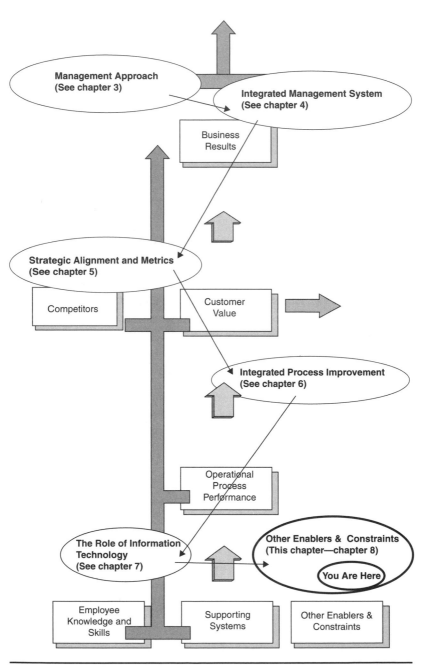

This navigational roadmap is intended to help readers understand the flow of information in these chapters and see how various topics fit into the overall model.

The extent to which constraints exist in an organization will be a large determinant of its capacity to successfully implement ongoing process improvement and change initiatives. Some organizations will have high levels of inertia to overcome and pose very high levels of risk to any change effort, while others have an environment that thrives on change. The same factors that act as constraints can be turned into enablers if the organization and the environment are designed and optimized for change.

In fact, what generally differentiates a factor from being either an enabler or a constraint is the alignment (or misalignment) with the organization's goals and strategy. Factors become constraints when they are out of alignment with the direction of the change the company wants to make. Viewing the entire organization (including these factors) as a system and developing an understanding of the relationship of these different areas to the performance of the "system" as a whole is essential.

Companies that invest in developing an environment where the culture and values, organizational structure and supporting systems, and rewards/ recognition for performance are all congruent with the company's overall vision and strategy will have a much easier task of implementing process improvement and reengineering efforts.

Plans for dealing with enablers and constraints should be well integrated into the process improvement initiative at the appropriate point, not treated as an afterthought to the project. In some cases, these factors may be very significant and require a considerable amount of focused effort and commitment.

For example, one of the key factors in successfully implementing a change management initiative that might be required to support a major redefinition of business processes is the creation of a sense of urgency and immediacy of the need for change.

> "The pain of the current state must be visible not only to outsiders, but widely accepted by senior managers within an organization. Often, consultants, the business press, and a handful of executives are aware that problems with key processes threaten a firm's long-term survival, but are unable to convince the majority of the firm's managers that radical corrective action is required."
>
> ". . . The trick, of course, is to convince an organization of the need for change before a crisis occurs—while there is still time to do something about it."[1]

CULTURAL AND BEHAVIORAL FACTORS

Many quality standards, such as ISO 9000, have not given sufficient attention to the human behavioral aspects of quality and business process improvement. Real quality comes from the heart . . . it comes from people who believe in what they are doing and take pride in doing it well. There has been a somewhat naive belief in some cases that if you just write an ISO procedure or work instruction, people will automatically follow it like robots. It rarely works that way in the real world. The implementation of any quality system needs to be sensitive to the human behavioral aspects of the system.

Regardless of whatever other cultural norms and values an organization may adopt, creating an environment that supports ongoing change is probably one of the most fundamental requirements. An ideal objective would be to include individuals and create teams across the organization who:[2]

- Accept change as a regular and expected feature of their business activities and have developed positive attitudes to change in their business culture

- Actively seek opportunities to introduce beneficial change

- Seek to disseminate information, not restrict it, to the benefit of other staff, clients, and suppliers

- Naturally and effectively consult fully with other team members, team leaders, and other teams

- Place emphasis on successful implementation of change as a measure of their personal success

- Are able to think strategically and act with tactical skill across a wide range of business situations

Systems' thinking is very important to achieving these goals. Peter Senge points out that if you look deeply into any complex human system, you will find infinite complexity and systems that are never completely understood.

"When a group of people collectively recognize that nobody has the answer, it transforms the quality of that organization in a remarkable way. And so we teach executives to live with uncertainty, because no matter how smart or successful you are, a fundamental uncertainty will always be present in your life. That fact creates a philosophic communality between people in an organization, which is usually accompanied by an enthusiasm for experimentation. If you are never going to get the answer, all you can do is experiment. When something goes wrong, it's no longer necessary to blame someone for screwing up—mistakes are simply part of the experiment."[3]

American culture and management style are also heavily influenced by a "command and control" philosophy, which is rooted in some of Frederick Taylor's early influences and Sloan's introduction of management by the numbers.[4] Dismantling the beliefs that: (1) people can control an organization from the top or at a distance, and (2) that you can ever fully understand a system or figure it out is essential to developing a "learning organization environment" that is optimized for continuous change.[5]

Both Senge and Davenport emphasize the importance of mental models and building a shared vision to develop the teamwork and collaboration that is essential to achieving effective process and organizational performance:

> "Successful leaders of transformational restructuring understand that changes in mental models, attitudes, values, and, ultimately, behavior are the foundation for successful implementation of these changes in operational and management structures and systems. They also understand that changes in mental models must precede changes in behavior. Greater cooperation between functional groups is an example of the kind of behavior that is almost always required to improve the performance of major organizational processes."[6]

Many companies have developed mission statements as a means of communicating the fundamental values and beliefs to all employees; however, for a mission statement to be effective, it must be more than a slogan. Kaplan and Norton talk about the role of a mission statement in their book on the Balanced Scorecard.

> "Mission statements should be inspirational. They should supply energy and motivation to the organization. But inspirational mission statements and slogans are not sufficient. As Peter Senge observed, 'Many leaders have personal visions that never get translated into shared visions that galvanize an organization. What has been lacking is a discipline for translating individual vision into shared vision.'"[7]

Beyond having a well-defined set of values, putting in place metrics that reinforce those values and that are consistently implemented throughout the company is also an important way to unify the company's direction. The Balanced Scorecard approach previously discussed provides a mechanism for translating mission and strategy into objectives and measures. Coupling the mission statement with measurable results and linking it with rewards and recognition is essential to provide substance to it and make it real.

AN EXAMPLE—SPRINT QUALITY SYSTEM

The extract below from the Sprint Quality System illustrates the kind of cultural values that are important to create an environment that supports continuous improvement.

Sprint Quality Essentials

Sprint believes that, at the core of conducting business successfully, these essentials must be in place:

Teamwork is essential for a large organization such as Sprint to operate effectively. The Sprint Quality Handbook, downloadable from our Resources area, presents a number of tools and techniques that help teams work effectively.

Strategic Integration is our method of meeting customer needs. It is essential for us to determine what our customers want, honestly evaluate what we currently provide them, and gain insight into any gap between the two. We then work toward closing this gap by improving our key processes.

Continuous Quality Improvement depends on individual and team efforts, since improvement often results from thousands of small efforts and a few breakthroughs.

We also need to continuously improve every aspect of our business. It is not acceptable to rest on a plateau or be merely "good enough." If we stop improving—or even slow down—while our competitors continue to improve, we are essentially falling behind.

Sprint Quality Principles

Sprint Quality includes four guiding beliefs or principles. These are:

Customer Focus—Becoming successful requires focusing on customers and understanding their needs.

Respect for People—People deserve respect and exhibit far higher performance when they receive it.

Management by Fact—Basing decisions and actions on fact, rather than speculation, produces far better business results.

Structured Problem Solving—Solving problems in an organized, systematic way greatly improves the chances of finding the best solution. [Download the Sprint Quality Handbook from the resources area (see Appendix B) to see some of the problem-solving tools used by Sprint associates.]

Sprint Values

The values we share at Sprint are tremendously important to all of us. By creating a set of values, we eliminate the need to write procedures for every possible situation that we will face in our business lives at Sprint.

Customer First—We anticipate, understand, meet, and exceed our customer's needs and expectations to achieve exceptional customer satisfaction.

Integrity In All We Do—Our actions and decisions reflect the highest ethical, legal, and professional standards.

Excellence Through Quality—We will individually and collectively use Sprint Quality in our daily activities to achieve excellence as a company.

Respect For Each Other—We care about our company, our work, our customers, and each other. This caring is a unique source of our company's energy, strength, and excellence.

Growth Through Change—We will grow as a company, as individuals, and as professionals by creating, anticipating, and responding to change.

Community Commitment—We willingly serve the charitable and civic needs of our communities.

Productive Work Environment—We provide a safe and accessible work environment.

Representative Work Force—We recruit and develop individuals who reflect the diversity of our communities.

Shareholder Value—We will increase shareholder value, build the financial strength of our company, and, as a result, prosper as individuals.[8]

The importance of the role of training, communications, and rewards and recognition in creating an environment and culture that supports these goals cannot be overlooked. The Sprint Quality System is a good example. It emphasizes empowering employees and providing tools to enable them to do their jobs more effectively rather than using a more prescriptive approach. All new employees are provided with training in the Sprint Quality System and a number of more advanced training courses on quality, leadership, problem-solving techniques, and other related skills are available through Sprint's "University of Excellence," as well as other formats such as computer-based training.

The following are some comments from Sprint employees regarding their training program. They reflect the level of significance of training as a factor in making the Sprint quality system successful. These quotes were extracted with permission from Sprint from their internal employee magazine that devoted an entire issue in March 2002 on their quality system:[9]

> "I've worked in various corporate settings and never encountered such a complete tool kit. It is packaged and ready for use on arrival. I constantly use the tools, especially the process documentation/flowcharts. They help problems become solutions."
> —Carol Kozloski, Manager Technology Services

> "Never underestimate the power of giving a new hire something as nice as a gold Sprint pin for completing the course. I make a presentation out of it, and it's great to see faces light up. Think about it . . . in most jobs, you wait five years to get any jewelry."
> —Michael Sizemore, Analyst III, Training and Technology Services

> "The course gave me the guidance and structure to organize my thoughts during my first weeks at work. I see the course as an effective and easy-to-understand source of essential tools for success. It beats spending months discovering the tools on your own."
> —Andrei Sobolevsky, Manager, Finance GMG

ORGANIZATIONAL STRUCTURE

Today's organizations are typically not well designed to maximize their effectiveness in meeting customer needs. Organizations are typically built around a functional structure that can inhibit the cross-functional collaboration that is needed. The linkages to integrate the senior management team responsible for defining the business strategy with ongoing process management and process improvement efforts in most organizations are also very weak (at best), as shown in Figure 8.1.

The typical missing link that is needed is to join the centers of expertise (information technology, process improvement, and quality management) with the functional management perspectives and to integrate the entire

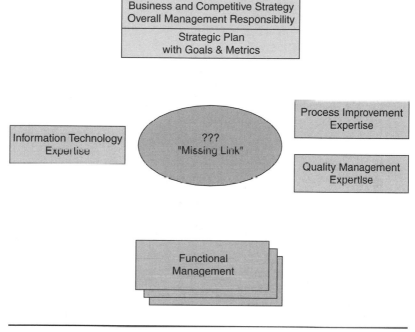

Figure 8.1 Typical organizational linkages.

effort with the higher-level strategic direction. Most of this problem is the need for a focal point to integrate these different approaches into the business strategy. The CEO of a company may be the only manager with sufficient cross-functional visibility across the organization to integrate the various perspectives required for effective implementation of improvement initiatives.

Creating a more integrated approach may require some new roles that do not currently exist in most organizations, as well as redefining the overall management structure and roles around a process orientation. At a minimum:

- All members of the senior management team need to assume more of a cross-functional perspective.

- A management focal point probably is needed to facilitate this group and further integrate the entire team.

Companies are moving to more horizontal, process-oriented organizations and flattening hierarchies to become more flexible and adaptive:

"There's an awful lot more productivity you're going to see in the next few years as we move to horizontally organized structures with a focus on the customer . . . Just as a light bulb wastes electricity to produce unwanted heat, a traditional corporation expends a tremendous amount of energy running its own internal machinery—managing relations among departments or providing information up and down the hierarchy, for example.

"A horizontal structure eliminates most of those tasks and focuses almost all of a company's resources on its customers. That's why proponents of the idea say it can deliver dramatic improvements in efficiency and speed."[10]

INFORMATION TECHNOLOGY

Information technology can be a significant constraint because it is so integral to the design of processes. In some cases, the overall information technology architecture may be a very broad-based constraint that affects process improvement throughout the entire company. In many of those situations, the costs and complexity of replacing these systems may be too great to undertake as part of an individual process improvement or reengineering effort, and the constraints imposed by continuing to operate within the current system may need to be considered in the project.

Enterprise resource planning (ERP) systems have radically changed the way people think about the relationship between business processes and information systems and will ultimately provide a much better foundation for managing ongoing change. There are several very critical tradeoffs associated with the selection and implementation of large-scale ERP systems:

1. Standardization and tight process control across a company have benefits in reducing the costs and complexity of the processes and associated systems, but it can make the company inflexible if it inhibits the ability to easily customize processes and systems to unique customer needs and requirements.

2. Adopting industry standard, best-in-class process blueprints reduces the costs of designing and maintaining unique processes and information systems, but could reduce or eliminate any competitive differentiation that a unique process might provide. (New technology is making it much easier to add on other best-in-class applications to an existing ERP system and mix-and-match a variety of applications as needed, rather than being locked into a single monolithic ERP system.)

3. Using a single ERP system for a range of applications across the whole company has advantages from an integration perspective, but involves a very high level of risk and may not be as optimal as individual point products that are designed for a particular function.

To effectively make these tradeoffs, companies need to differentiate processes and systems that are critical to providing competitive advantage, as well as those that require flexibility to adapt to unique customer needs and requirements. There are typically some systems in companies that can easily be standardized without losing any competitive differentiation and without significantly affecting flexibility to respond to unique customer requirements. An appropriate compromise might be an architecture that provides standardization and control for less critical business processes and still allows the flexibility to use other applications that are optimized for specific functions and have more flexibility to adapt to unique requirements.

For example, there is probably a lot to gain and not much to lose from standardizing and controlling accounting systems for tracking costs and manufacturing systems for control of materials and the production process. However, a company that does a lot of custom project business might want to provide a higher level of flexibility to project managers for developing unique project plans for individual customer requirements, and to use different tools with the ability to exchange information and data with the core business systems.

Another advantage of this approach would be to be able to quickly prototype and evolve processes and systems on the "periphery" without disrupting the core business processes at the core of the business. As some of these processes become proven and mature, and there is benefit to be gained from standardization, they can be assimilated into the core. This type of approach has been difficult to implement in the past; however, new technology is rapidly evolving to make it a much more practical alternative (see chapter 7).

ENDNOTES

1. T. H. Davenport, *Process Innovation* (Cambridge, MA: Harvard Business School Press, 1993): 171–73.
2. D. Lyneham-Brown, "Making Change the Culture," *Management Services* (October 1997): 39.
3. P. Senge, "Systems Thinking," *Executive Excellence* (January 1996): 15.
4. J. Soddon, "Thinking System Performance," *Management Services* (September 1997): 18–19.

5. Ibid.

6. See note 1: 175–76.

7. R. S. Kaplan and D. P. Norton, *The Balanced Scorecard* (Cambridge, MA: Harvard Business School Press, 1996): 24.

8. "Sprint Quality Approach," www.sprint.com/sprint/values/quality/approach.html.

9. "Hooked on Sprint Quality," *The Point for all Sprint Employees* (March 2002): 3.

10. J. A. Byrne, "The Horizontal Corporation," *Business Week* (October 20, 1993): 77–78.

9

Putting it All Together

CHAPTER OVERVIEW

Companies are at different stages of maturity in implementing many of the concepts that have been discussed in this book, and an action plan for further development will depend on what level of maturity the company has already achieved.

This chapter discusses a maturity model that can be used to understand the current level of maturity of an existing management system, determine what level of maturity would be desirable, and develop an action plan to reach the higher level.

PROCESS IMPROVEMENT "ROADMAP"

It is important to recognize that companies are at different levels of maturity in implementing these concepts, and it does not necessarily make sense to make a huge jump from a very low level of maturity to a very complex and sophisticated approach. That lesson has been well understood in the software development industry for a long time and has been implemented in the SEI/CMM model (Software Engineering Institute Capability Maturity Model).[1] It defines levels of maturity associated with a software development process and characteristics of each level for five different levels of maturity:

- It provides a very useful tool for organizations to understand their current level of maturity and a progression that would lead to higher levels of maturity.

- By developing an understanding of the difficulty as well as the benefits of achieving a given level of maturity, organizations can make a conscious decision of what level of maturity makes the most sense for their current needs. Very few organizations make it all the way to level five, for example, because it is extremely difficult to achieve.

A similar model can be developed to better understand levels of maturity of a business system and can be used to help companies develop an action plan based on their current level of maturity and desired future state:

- The maturity of the company's business environment will have an impact on its ability to successfully implement process improvement efforts (either incremental or radical).

- Similarly, an effort to improve processes is probably futile if the very basic elements that are needed to support effective process management are not in place.

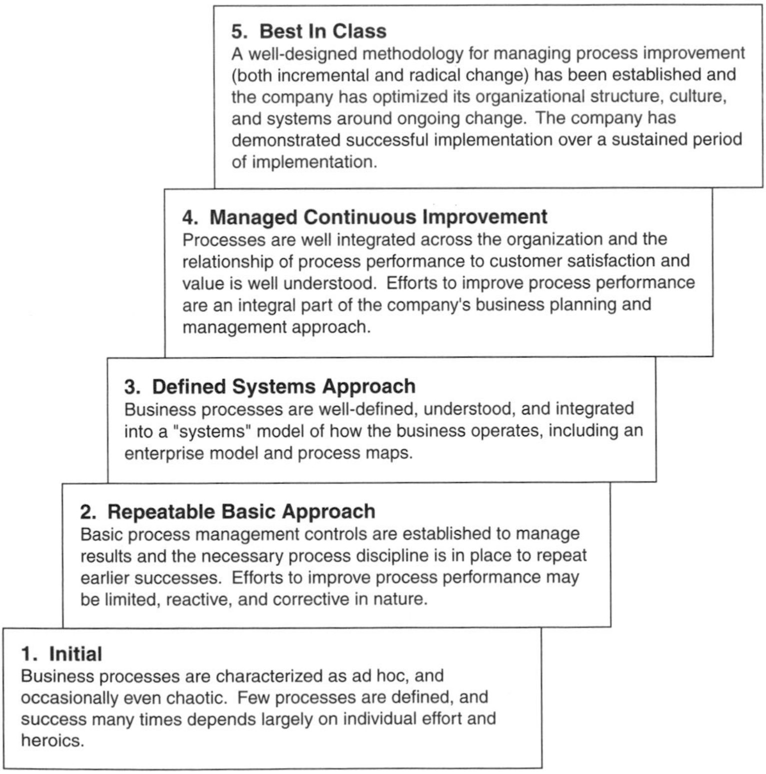

5. Best In Class
A well-designed methodology for managing process improvement (both incremental and radical change) has been established and the company has optimized its organizational structure, culture, and systems around ongoing change. The company has demonstrated successful implementation over a sustained period of implementation.

4. Managed Continuous Improvement
Processes are well integrated across the organization and the relationship of process performance to customer satisfaction and value is well understood. Efforts to improve process performance are an integral part of the company's business planning and management approach.

3. Defined Systems Approach
Business processes are well-defined, understood, and integrated into a "systems" model of how the business operates, including an enterprise model and process maps.

2. Repeatable Basic Approach
Basic process management controls are established to manage results and the necessary process discipline is in place to repeat earlier successes. Efforts to improve process performance may be limited, reactive, and corrective in nature.

1. Initial
Business processes are characterized as ad hoc, and occasionally even chaotic. Few processes are defined, and success many times depends largely on individual effort and heroics.

Figure 9.1 Management system maturity model.

- Companies need to implement effective quality management and process management systems before any serious improvement initiative is considered.

Figure 9.1 shows a potential maturity model that can be used to evaluate the maturity of a business management system.

Table 9.1 shows examples of how these stages of maturity apply to typical management systems.

This model is not meant to imply a fixed and rigid progression; however, the risks of any company attempting to make a quantum leap in process maturity by bypassing some of the intermediate steps need to be understood. Figure 9.2 shows the characteristics that might typically be found at each level of this maturity model.

Assessing the Maturity of a Management System

The management system is essential to provide the environment and framework for effectively managing any individual process improvement or reengineering initiatives. Figure 9.3 is an example of a high-level assessment model for evaluating the maturity of a quality/business system.

How to Use this Model

Although this type of assessment model is far from exact, it can provide:

- A good high-level assessment of the maturity of a company's management system

- An identification of strengths and weaknesses in the management system approach to prioritize areas for improvement

The model also helps identify inconsistencies that might inhibit full performance at any level of maturity. For example, an attempt to implement Six Sigma as a process improvement methodology (Level 4) might have limited success if the management approach and process management model is still at Level 2.

DEVELOPING AN ACTION PLAN

Here are a few suggested guidelines for developing an action plan of "what to do next":

Table 9.1 Maturity Level Examples.

Current Maturity Level	Example	Primary Actions Needed for Next Level
1. Initial Business processes are characterized as ad hoc, and occasionally even chaotic. Few processes are defined, and success many times depends largely on individual effort and heroics.	• The company has no defined management system and/or quality standards are not effectively used. • "Firefighting" to control problems is prevalent in the company. **This level is similar to having no defined quality management system or to a superficial and ineffective implementation of the ISO 9000 requirements.**	***Move up to level 2:*** • Implement basic quality management system or improve the effectiveness of current system implementation.
2. Repeatable basic approach Basic process management controls are established to manage results and the necessary process discipline is in place to repeat earlier successes. Efforts to improve process performance may be limited, reactive, and corrective in nature.	• The company has implemented a basic quality management system. Processes are defined and repeatable and basic process discipline is in place. • Quality management may not be well integrated with business management and the approach may be primarily reactive and corrective. • Within individual processes, procedures are defined. However, there may not be an overall systems model of the business (enterprise models and process maps) and management of individual processes and the enterprise may not be fully integrated. **This level is similar to an *effective* implementation of the ISO 9000:1994 requirements**	***Move up to level 3:*** • Implement basic continuous improvement capability similar to ISO 9000:2000. • Create process maps to define all processes. • Identify key metrics for each process and implement management review process. • Provide at least a limited level of engagement of senior management staff in management review process.

Continued

Table 9.1		*Continued*
Current Maturity Level	**Example**	**Primary Actions Needed for Next Level**
3. Defined Systems Approach Business processes are well defined, understood, and integrated into a "systems" model of how the business operates, including an enterprise model and process maps.	The company has implemented a very effective quality system that includes an emphasis on continuous improvement: • Comprehensive metrics may not be in place and process improvement initiatives may not be fully integrated and aligned with business goals. • Management emphasis is primarily at the process level and the overall system may not be completely integrated to include both quality and business management functions. • A basic improvement methodology is in place. **This level is similar to an effective implementation of the ISO 9000:2000 standard.**	***Move up to Level 4:*** • Begin integrating quality system with business objectives. • Define overall enterprise model, mission, vision, and objectives and engage all levels of management in the effort. • Implement a planned and proactive approach to continuous improvement (Six Sigma or equivalent). • Define metrics to support the overall model and identify linkages between process level metrics, customer satisfaction, and business results. • Ensure that information systems and other enablers and constraints are well-aligned with achieving organizational goals and results. • Define overall assessment model and implement a value-added assessment process to support continuous improvement goals.

Table 9.1 *Continued*

Current Maturity Level	Example	Primary Actions Needed for Next Level
4. Managed Continuous Improvement Processes are well integrated across the organization and the relationship of process performance to customer satisfaction and value is well understood. Efforts to improve process performance are an integral part of the company's business planning and management approach.	• The company has fully integrated their quality and process improvement initiatives into an overall business management strategy that is effectively implemented across the entire company with a very effective system of comprehensive metrics. • The management emphasis of the system is planned and proactive rather than reactive and corrective. • An effective improvement methodology similar to Six Sigma is in place (may be implemented as a "program" and not fully integrated with business management system). **This level would meet all the requirements of the ISO 9000:2000 standard as well as basic implementation of the Baldrige criteria.**	*Move up to Level 5:* • Develop a high level of cross-functional integration among all managers. Create a culture and environment backed up by very strong leadership that supports ongoing continuous improvement. • Define and implement a systems approach to managing the business based on a solid understanding of the overall business and individual processes. • Develop assessment models that effectively integrate all required standards and best practices and train assessors as value-added process consultants. • Fully integrate all metrics at all levels (Balanced Scorecard or equivalent approach). • Develop an integrated approach to process improvement that includes provision for process reengineering as well as incremental improvement, and effectively integrates advanced use of technology and IT systems design with the design of the business processes.

Table 9.1

Current Maturity Level	Example	Primary Actions Needed for Next Level
5. Best In Class A well-designed methodology for managing process improvement (both incremental and radical change) has been established and the company has optimized its organizational structure, culture, and systems around ongoing change. The company has demonstrated successful implementation over a sustained period of implementation.	• All functions and processes in the organization are well-integrated around a common set of goals and objectives and there is a very high level of cross-functional collaboration throughout the organization. • A well-integrated and effective improvement methodology is in place that considers the need for reengineering as well as incremental improvement. The improvement methodology is well aligned and integrated with driving business results. • The design and implementation of information systems is well-integrated with the design of business processes, and advanced information technology plays a very key role in leveraging high levels of business results. • A comprehensive and well integrated system of metrics (similar to the Balanced Scorecard) has been implemented throughout the business and is used as an integration mechanism to fully integrate process management and process improvement initiatives with higher level business results and customer value metrics **The company has a very sophisticated systems approach to managing the business and is able to quickly and easily assimilate any new standards and best practices as needed.**	

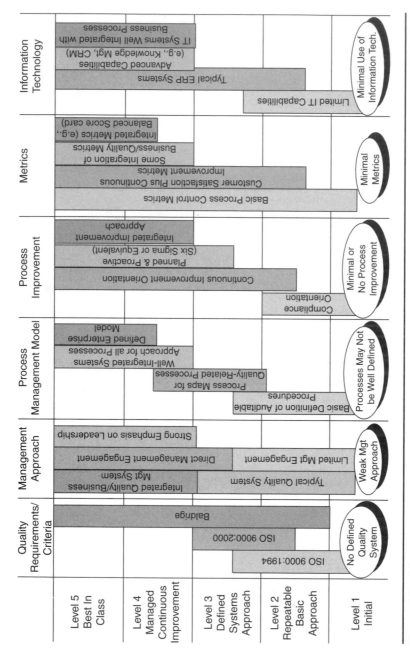

Figure 9.2 Management system maturity levels.

- Use the business process maturity model in Figure 9.1 and Table 9.1 to identify where your business is in terms of having a well-integrated quality/business management system.

- Complete the "Management System Maturity Survey" in Figure 9.3 and use the information in Figure 9.2 to make a determination of where your business is and where you might need to improve. A good idea is to involve the company's senior management team in this process so that the result is a cross-functional consensus view.

- From the information above, develop consensus on the areas of weakness in the management system maturity survey that would have the greatest impact on the business and develop an action plan to address these areas (see Figure 9.4).

Of course, the action plan will depend on what the area of weakness is; however, here are some specific suggestions to consider including in your action plan (the desired goal is to implement projects that help close the gap with the next highest level of maturity):

1. Determine where the company currently is in terms of management system maturity as discussed above and identify the desired level of where the company would like to be. (Be realistic about how big a jump is reasonable in a given amount of time.)

2. In addition to the basic and cursory assessment discussed above, a much more detailed "gap assessment" is needed to help define an action plan (see Appendix B for a description of a software tool that can be used for this purpose):

   - Create an assessment model that is designed around the needs of the business (rather than compliance with a particular standard) and is consistent with the "desired level" identified above. Include criteria from all relevant standards and industry best practices and gain consensus on the model among the senior management team.

   - Perform a detailed gap assessment against the assessment model to identify areas of weakness and prioritize the findings.

3. Do not overlook the need for training. Training plays an extremely important role in not only understanding the management system model, but also building consensus and commitment.

4. Tools and information systems are an essential and inseparable part of a good action plan and should be an integral part of the plan.

How effectively does your management system meet the following criteria:	NA	Poor			Average			Excellent		
Criteria:	0	1	2	3	4	5	6	7	8	9
1. We have a well-defined system model of how our business functions that is understood throughout the company and is used as an important business management tool	▣	▣	▣	▣	▣	▣	▣	▣	▣	▣
2. Our management system effectively integrates the latest version of all standards and other best practices that may be relevant to our business	▣	▣	▣	▣	▣	▣	▣	▣	▣	▣
3. Our management system is well aligned with our business goals through appropriate metrics that are an integral part of the way the business is managed	▣	▣	▣	▣	▣	▣	▣	▣	▣	▣
4. Our management system has a focus on continuous improvement and includes all aspects of business effectiveness and customer satisfaction	▣	▣	▣	▣	▣	▣	▣	▣	▣	▣
5. Our assessment approach is perceived as value-added and provides important feedback to managers on areas for improvement at both a system and process level	▣	▣	▣	▣	▣	▣	▣	▣	▣	▣
6. We have an effectively designed methodology (Six Sigma or equivalent) for managing improvement initiatives that is well integrated into our overall quality management system	▣	▣	▣	▣	▣	▣	▣	▣	▣	▣
7. Our information systems and tools used in support of our quality management system are well designed to help us become more effective and minimize resource utilization	▣	▣	▣	▣	▣	▣	▣	▣	▣	▣

Figure 9.3   Management system maturity survey.   *Continued*

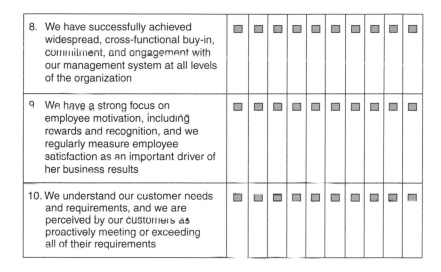

8. We have successfully achieved widespread, cross-functional buy-in, commitment, and engagement with our management system at all levels of the organization	□	□	□	□	□	□	□	□	□	□
9. We have a strong focus on employee motivation, including rewards and recognition, and we regularly measure employee satisfaction as an important driver of her business results	□	□	□	□	□	□	□	□	□	□
10. We understand our customer needs and requirements, and we are perceived by our customers as proactively meeting or exceeding all of their requirements	□	□	□	□	□	□	□	□	□	□

Figure 9.3 *Continued*

5. Cross-functional participation with strong senior management support is also essential to ensure successful execution of the action plan. A steering group consisting of representatives of all organizations that have a role in implementing the plan or that may be impacted by the plan is critical.

Figure 9.4 shows an example of a high-level planning process that can be used to develop this action plan.

Roles and Responsibilities

The following is a general description of some of the roles and responsibilities that may be needed to make this model work (these are intended only as general guidelines and are not meant to be prescriptive):

1. Senior Management Leadership

   The top-level management function in the company plays a very critical role in steering the direction of process improvement and reengineering efforts to achieve the company's strategy and goals, yet many companies are not well organized to fulfill that role. What is needed is to:

   • Develop a management approach for all senior managers based on the principles described in chapter 3.

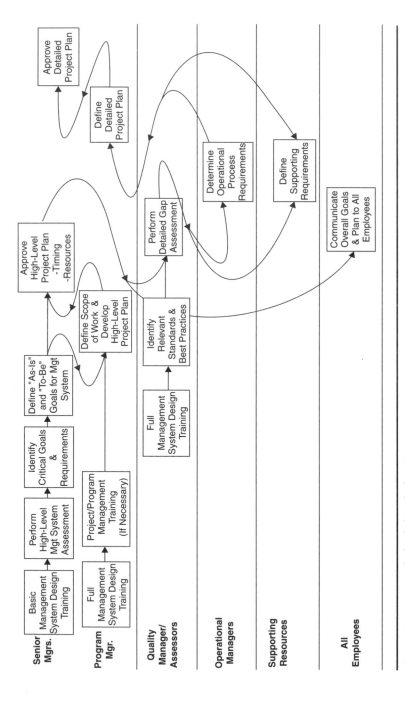

Figure 9.4   Example high-level planning process.

- Define a strategic plan with appropriate goals and metrics and review progress against both short-term tactical business management goals and longer-term process improvement requirements linked to the mission and vision for the organization (see chapter 4).

- Design a management system that is oriented around implementing that concept as described in chapter 5, including as necessary:

  - Enterprise models to understand how the company operates as a system

  - Process mapping to provide a more detailed understanding of the operation of critical business processes

  - Lifecycle models defined as needed to manage technology and market trends, products, and projects

The distinction between leadership and management must be clearly understood and the level of leadership engagement that is needed is more than just providing support.

2. Management Focal Point and Program Manager

A management focal point is needed to plan, coordinate, and manage process improvement and reengineering efforts within the company. This role does not currently exist in many companies. The skills required span several traditional organizations (quality management, IS management, and so on) and none of these organizations typically has the complete range of skills needed.

This role needs to be perceived as objective and independent of any one functional organization and, for that reason, may need to be defined as a new role. The people to fill this management role may come from a quality management, IS, strategic planning, or reengineering background. Typically, none of those organizations individually has the skills required, and it will take time to develop people with the cross-disciplinary focus that is needed to fill that role. What is important is to objectively define the skills required and to make it an independent role with a sufficient level of management influence.

3. Program/Project Management

Many companies develop excellent business strategies and goals but fail to develop an adequate level of project management, resources, and focus to successfully manage and implement the initiative required to support the plan. If a company is focused on static quality control, that may be sufficient; however, in an organization that is designed for ongoing continuous improvement, it must be able to successfully manage a portfolio or improvement initiatives. Effective, cross-functional project management is essential to that.

The following checklists of requirements for successful project implementation has been adapted from *Corporate Renaissance* and *Process Innovation* (these items would be appropriate for a team implementing a new, integrated quality and management system; a streamlined version of these same checklist items could be used for less complex projects).[2]

Program/Project Management Checklist:

- *Clear ownership of the effort is established at the senior management level.*

- *Mission, goals, and objectives are clearly articulated.*

- *A full-time project manager is assigned.*

Project Team Checklist:

- *The project team must reflect appropriate/required skills, perspectives, and knowledge.*

- *Stakeholder analysis should identify individuals and groups who are likely to be affected*—whenever possible, key stakeholders should be assigned to project teams.

- *Cross-functional representation is essential to ensure that a variety of perspectives are brought to bear.* Organizational representation also must be considered—change targets must be represented directly, both for their functional knowledge and to ensure buy-in.

- *Team members must grasp strategic realities as well as possess an operational understanding of the business.*

- *Team members must be trained in the techniques that will be used in the course of the effort.* Training should include problem solving, process documentation, and group dynamics.

- *Change management resources should be represented on a process innovation team where there is significant change required.* The role of the change management resources is to anticipate and mitigate the impact of changes that are implied in the project that might impede its success.

Project Plan Checklist:

- *A sound methodology and plan is defined and systematically followed.* A methodology and project plan should be established and documented during the initial start-up phase of the project to define the overall project management scheme, design methodologies, the implementation approach, and any other critical project requirements. The methodology should be consistent with the goals and objectives of the project, and appropriate for successfully managing the complexity and risk of the project.

- *A timetable/budget is established at the beginning of the project.* The project plan should clearly define the scope and goals of the project, as well as the major design and implementation requirements at a sufficient level of detail to estimate resources, schedule, and budget. The project plan should also identify potential risks, issues, and dependencies that must be overcome for successful completion.

- *Quantifiable success measures are defined and measured.* The project should have a quantifiable method of measuring progress, and a well-defined method for evaluating project success that is agreed on by all project team members and stakeholders.

Davenport has identified five factors that are essential to characterizing the scope and complexity of a process improvement or reengineering project (these factors are useful in determining the project approach that will be needed to achieve the desired results):[3]

1. Overall magnitude of change required
2. Level of uncertainty about change outcomes
3. Breadth of the change across and between organizations
4. Required depth of penetration of individual attitudes and behaviors
5. Duration of the change process

These factors are often overlooked or underestimated—the project plan should carefully consider their impact on the project management approach, methodology, resources, costs, and schedule to develop a realistic plan.

ENDNOTES

1. Carneghie Mellon University Software Engineering Institute, *The Capability Maturity Model: Guidelines for Improving the Software Process* (Reading, MA: Addison-Wesley Publishing, 1995).
2. K. Cross, J. Feather, and R. L. Lynch, *Corporate Renaissance* (Cambridge, MA: Blackwell Business, 1994): 27; T. H. Davenport, *Process Innovation* (Cambridge, MA: Harvard Business School Press, 1993): 183–86.
3. Ibid., 171.

10

Keeping the Progress Moving

CHAPTER OVERVIEW

Once an integrated management system is in place, keeping it moving forward is essential to provide for ongoing continuous improvement. For an organization that has been used to a static, compliance-oriented quality management system, this can be a significant change and a shift in thinking.

This chapter provides an overview of the fundamental requirements to shift to a management system that is oriented toward continuous improvement to sustain the forward progress that has been developed earlier.

Two very important elements must be in place to keep the progress moving forward:

1. Self-Assessment Approach

   Some form of self-assessment has always been an essential part of any quality management system. One of the most critical functions associated with developing, implementing, and continually improving integrated business and quality systems is determining how to assess the effectiveness of the system. The organization needs to be able to look at itself objectively and determine if all elements of the system are working as they should be to meet the goal of improving quality, customer satisfaction, and overall effectiveness.

   Most modern quality standards, such as the year 2000 version of the ISO 9000 family of standards, have shifted their emphasis away from pure compliance with requirements to more of a continuous improvement orientation. Even though these standards have shifted their focus, many auditors (both external and internal) have not changed their auditing approach significantly from the old style compliance orientation because that approach has been so engrained in the implementation of the ISO 9000 family of standards in the past.

A very different approach to auditing (assessment is a more appropriate term) is needed to support a continuous improvement orientation. The typical ISO 9000 audit approach that is designed to enforce compliance with the standard does not work well for continuous improvement. It typically does not provide sufficient information on opportunities for improvement that might go beyond meeting the minimum requirements of the standard and help the business or improve customer satisfaction and business results.

2. Goals and Metrics

A fundamental shift in thinking is needed in this area. Quality management systems that were typically associated with the 1994 version of the ISO 9000 standard had no specific requirements for continuous improvement. These systems were primarily oriented around static quality control and emphasized control of defects. In a continuous improvement environment, static quality control is no longer sufficient. The organization must continuously "raise the bar" by setting goals and metrics to improve performance and effectiveness, and the assessment approach must include evaluating progress against improvement goals.

AN ASSESSMENT APPROACH FOR CONTINUOUS IMPROVEMENT

The Role of the Assessor

In an assessment approach designed for continuous improvement, the roles of the participants need to change significantly. In a compliance auditing approach, there is typically a high level of reliance on the internal and external auditors to make the system work, as shown in Figure 10.1. The internal and external auditors are many times perceived as the "enforcers" of the requirements of the standard.

In a continuous improvement assessment approach, those roles need to shift, as shown in Figure 10.2. Relying on the internal and external auditors to make the system work typically is not effective. The responsibility has to

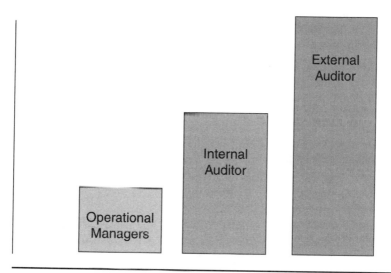

Figure 10.1   Typical perceived importance of compliance auditing roles.

be primarily on the operational managers themselves to make it work; the internal auditors (assessors) play more of a value-added consulting role to help identify opportunities for improvement, and the external auditors play a less significant role in validating that the overall system meets fundamental compliance requirements.

Metrics are essential to make this work. If the operational process managers have goals to improve their quality and operational performance, they should see the role of the assessors as essential to help them meet those goals and identify areas for improvement.

Evaluating Effectiveness

Any assessment approach that is designed to support continuous improvement must be more than a "pass/fail" compliance test. The assessment must provide value-added feedback to the operational managers who are responsible for the process being evaluated to help them understand its level of effectiveness as well as potential areas for further improvement. Any assessment that does that is naturally going to involve more of a subjective judgment than a typical compliance approach.

To mitigate the subjectivity, a team of assessors is typically used. The team discusses areas of inconsistency to reach consensus on an overall evaluation result. Guidelines for the evaluation also help provide some

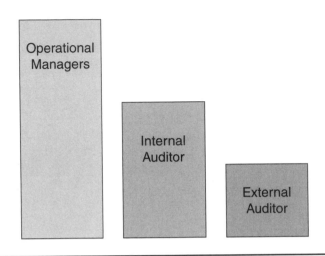

Figure 10.2 Typical perceived importance of continuous improvement assessment roles.

level of consistency in the findings. For example, a Baldrige examination rates two primary factors depending on the type of criteria being evaluated:

- Approach/Deployment

- Results

Approach/Deployment
"Approach/Deployment" evaluates the relative degree of an approach that satisfies the requirements of the criteria that have been identified, planned, defined, and implemented.

"Approach" refers to how you address the item requirements—the method used. The factors used to evaluate approaches include:[1]

- The appropriateness of the methods to the requirements

- The effectiveness of use of the methods and the degree to which the approach:

  - Is repeatable, integrated, and consistently applied

  - Embodies evaluation/improvement learning cycles

  - Is based on reliable information and data

- Alignment with your organizational needs

- Evidence of beneficial innovation and change

"Deployment" refers to the extent to which your approach is applied. The factors used to evaluate deployment include:[2]

- Use of the approach in addressing item requirements relevant and important to your organization

- Use of the approach by all appropriate work units

A Baldrige assessment uses the evaluation scales shown in Table 10.1 to evaluate the level of approach/deployment. (Note the values shown are based on the 2002 Baldrige criteria and change from year to year.)

Results

"Results" evaluates the effectiveness of the actual implementation of this requirement in achieving its goal. "Results" refers to outcomes in achieving the requirements. The factors used to evaluate results include:[3]

- Your current performance

- Your performance relative to appropriate comparisons and/or benchmarks

- Rate and breadth of your performance improvements

- Linkage of your results measures to important customer, market, process, and action plan performance requirements

The standard values for rating the results factor are defined in Table 10.2.

The Role of an Assessment Model

An *assessment model* is to a business/quality management system as a *functional specification* is to a complex software system. It defines the functions that the system must perform to be successful (critical success factors) and some of the basic design requirements the processes need to satisfy to successfully perform those functional requirements.

In a compliance-oriented environment or a very basic quality system, it is typically very simple; the assessment model is the quality standard that the quality system must comply with (for example, ISO 9000). In many cases, the scope of these requirements has been limited to the set of requirements that were auditable by quality auditors to meet the requirements of the standard.

There are many common implementation problems:

- Companies develop superficial quality systems that are only designed to satisfy the auditors and add little or no real value to the

Table 10.1   2003 Baldrige approach/deployment ratings.

Score (%)	Guidelines
0%	• No systematic approach is evident; information is anecdotal
10–20%	• The beginning of a systematic approach to the basic requirements of the Item is evident • Major gaps exist in deployment that would inhibit progress in achieving the basic requirements of the Item • Early stages of a transition from reacting to problems to a general improvement orientation are evident
30–40%	• An effective, systematic approach, responsive to the basic requirements of the Item, is evident • The approach is deployed, although some areas or work units are in early stages of deployment • The beginning of a systematic approach to evaluation and improvement of basic Item processes is evident
50–60%	• An effective, systematic approach, responsive to the overall requirements of the Item and your key business requirements, is evident • The approach is well deployed, although deployment may vary in some areas or work units • A fact-based, systematic evaluation and improvement process is in place for improving the efficiency and effectiveness of key processes • The approach is aligned with your basic organizational needs identified in the other Criteria categories
70–80%	• An effective, systematic approach, responsive to the multiple requirements of the Item and your current and changing business needs, is evident • The approach is well deployed, with no significant gaps • A fact-based, systematic evaluation and improvement process and organizational learning/sharing are key management tools; there is clear evidence of refinement and improved integration as a result of organizational-level analysis and sharing • The approach is well integrated with your organizational needs identified in the other Criteria categories
90–100%	• An effective, systematic approach, fully responsive to all the requirements of the Item and all your current and changing business needs, is evident • The approach is fully deployed without significant weaknesses or gaps in any areas or work units • A very strong, fact-based, systematic evaluation and improvement process and extensive organizational learning/sharing are key management tools; strong refinement and integration, backed by excellent organizational-level analysis and sharing, are evident • The approach is fully integrated with your organizational needs identified in the other Criteria categories

Baldrige National Quality Program, *2002 Criteria for Performance Excellence.*

Table 10.2   Baldrige results ratings.

Score (%)	Guidelines
0%	• There are no results or poor results in areas reported
10–20%	• There are some improvements and/or early good performance levels • Results are not reported for many to most areas of importance to your organization's key business requirements
30–40%	• Improvements and/or good performance levels are reported in many areas of importance to your organization's key business requirements • Early stages of developing trends and obtaining comparative information are evident • Results are reported for many to most areas of importance to your organization's key business requirements
50–60%	• Improvement trends and/or good performance levels are reported for most areas of importance to your organization's key business requirements • No pattern of adverse trends and no poor performance levels are evident in areas of importance to your organization's key business requirements • Some trends and/or current performance levels evaluated against relevant comparisons and/or benchmarks show areas of strength and/or good to very good relative performance levels • Business results address most key customer, market, and process requirements
70–80%	• Current performance is good to excellent in areas of importance to your organization's key business requirements • Most improvement trends and/or current performance levels are sustained • Many to most trends and/or current performance levels evaluated against relevant comparisons and/or benchmarks show areas of leadership and very good relative performance levels • Business results address most key customer, market, process, and action plan requirements
90–100%	• Current performance is excellent in most areas of importance to your organization's key business requirements • Excellent improvement trends and/or sustained excellent performance levels are reported in most areas • Evidence of industry and benchmark leadership is demonstrated in many areas; business results fully address key customer, market, process, and action plan requirements

business. It is unfortunate that this type of quality system has given ISO 9000 a bad reputation; the fault is not with the standard, it is in the implementation.

- Companies do not take the time to interpret what a standard means to their business and redefine or clarify the requirement as needed in the context of their business. Many times the quality manual simply "mimics" what is in the standard.

- Many quality manuals do not integrate business requirements that are considered "outside of the quality system." A good quality system should be well-integrated with achieving business results or it will probably add little value to the business.

In a continuous improvement environment, an assessment model may go well beyond basic compliance requirements. For example, it might be very reasonable to integrate some of the requirements of the Baldrige criteria with the requirements of the ISO 9000 standard to create an integrated assessment model for continuous improvement. A good assessment model might also include criteria, compliance requirements, and best practices from a number of different sources not limited to quality standards. For example:

- Environmental standards, security standards, health and safety standards

- Information technology standards and requirements

- Financial management standards and requirements (accounting practices)

- Best practices from lessons learned in the industry

The important point is that if the goal is to design systems for effectiveness and continuous improvement, the assessment model should not be limited to a single set of compliance requirements. The assessment model provides a framework for assessing the effectiveness of the business and quality management system. If the assessment model is not well designed, it will be difficult to implement an effective assessment approach.

An Example Assessment Approach

As an example, an assessment tool has been created to demonstrate this overall approach. (See Appendix B for instructions on downloading a free evaluation copy of the software.) The tool provides several important areas of functionality:

1. Customized Assessment Models

    It makes it easy to define unique assessment models from a number of different sources. For example, Baldrige criteria can be mixed with ISO 9000 requirements to create a customized model:

    - Point values can be assigned to the criteria in the model to create a scoring system similar to Baldrige.

    - Criteria can be rated in terms of importance to the organization and in terms of difficulty to make further progress in order to prioritize assessment results for reporting purposes.

2. Continuous Improvement Assessment Framework

    The tool uses a modified version of the Baldrige framework for assessment. In addition to the standard Baldrige rating criteria for Approach/Deployment and Results, the tool adds the capability to rate the importance and difficulty, as shown in Figures 10.3 through 10.5.

3. Achieving Consensus Among Assessors

    The tool allows a team of assessors to easily compare their findings to resolve inconsistencies and reach consensus on an overall evaluation, as shown in Figure 10.6.

4. Prioritizing an Action Plan

    In a continuous improvement assessment, there are often many more opportunities for improvement than can be done within a given amount of resources and the assessment tool provides a capability to rank assessment findings in a variety of ways to prioritize areas for improvement. Figure 10.7 shows a report of an assessment by level of importance. This report shows the areas of highest importance to the organization with the weakest approach and deployment score.

THE ROLE OF METRICS

Metrics play a very important role in developing a good assessment approach that is designed to evaluate the effectiveness of continuous improvement systems, but metrics in themselves are only indicators and are not sufficient in many cases to diagnose systemic problems. They also do not provide design guidelines of how the system must be designed to

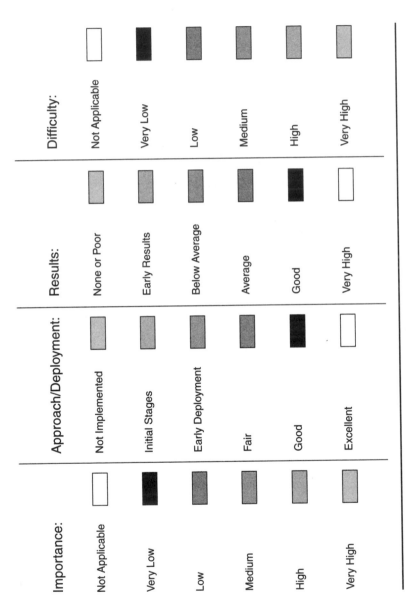

Figure 10.3 Example assessment rating criteria.

Rating	Percent Value	Guidelines
Not Applicable	0%	No impact on quality/customer satisfaction and/or company's business results
Very Low	10–20%	Very limited impact on quality/customer satisfaction and/or company's business results
Low	30–40%	Low impact on quality/customer satisfaction and/or company's business results
Medium	50–60%	Medium impact on quality/customer satisfaction and/or company's business results
High	70–80%	High impact on quality/customer satisfaction and/or company's business results
Very High	90–100%	Very high impact on quality/customer satisfaction and/or company's business results

Figure 10.4   Example importance ratings.

achieve the metrics goals. Metrics and requirements go hand-in-hand; ideally one complements the other.

Metrics lead the assessor to look in the right area and they help focus the assessment on areas that have an impact on customer satisfaction and business results. Without this kind of data, the assessment might focus on trivial compliance issues that have little or no relation to what's important to customers and the business.

A Baldrige assessment approach is typically a "top-down" approach. It starts with the company's business objectives and looks down into the organization for alignment of all of the factors that would support achieving those objectives. An ISO 9000 assessment is typically more of a horizontal process assessment and looks at a particular process to determine if the process is operating effectively based on whatever metrics and requirements are appropriate to that process.

Rating	Percent Value	Guidelines
Not Applicable	0%	No need to address this area
Very Low	10–20%	Very low level of difficulty to demonstrate further improvement in this area
Low	30–40%	Low level of difficulty to demonstrate further improvement in this area
Medium	50–60%	Medium level of difficulty to demonstrate further improvement in this area
High	70–80%	High level of difficulty to demonstrate further improvement in this area
Very High	90–100%	Very high level of difficulty to demonstrate further improvement in this area

Figure 10.5   Example difficulty ratings.

Category/ SubCategory	Assessor	Importance	Approach Deployment	Results	Difficulty
Management Responsibilty					
Quality Policy					
	Jim Smith	5.0	2.0	1.0	2.0
	Joe Johnson	1.0	5.0	5.0	5.0
4.1.1	*Quality Policy*	**3.0**	**3.5**	**3.0**	**3.5**
	Jim Smith	5.0	0.0	0.0	3.0
	Joe Johnson	5.0	0.0	0.0	3.0
4.1.1.C.1	*Quality Objectives*	**5.0**	**0.0**	**0.0**	**3.0**
	Quality Policy	**4.0**	**1.8**	**1.5**	**3.3**

Figure 10.6   Example report used to reach consensus.

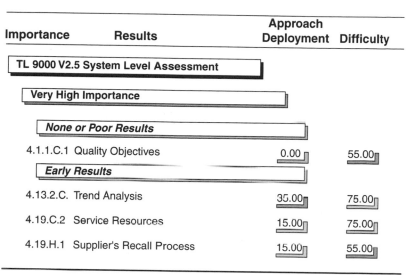

Importance	Results	Approach Deployment	Difficulty
TL 9000 V2.5 System Level Assessment			
Very High Importance			
None or Poor Results			
4.1.1.C.1 Quality Objectives		0.00	55.00
Early Results			
4.13.2.C. Trend Analysis		35.00	75.00
4.19.C.2 Service Resources		15.00	75.00
4.19.H.1 Supplier's Recall Process		15.00	55.00

Figure 10.7   Example report assessment findings by importance.

System-level Metrics Example

System-level metrics that indicate the overall performance of the business system against key goals and objectives can provide an important indicator of how well the business is doing and help focus the assessment on areas of the business that will create the maximum impact. A Baldrige assessment, for example, will typically start by looking at the company's strategic plan to determine what the company considers to be its most important business objectives and look for measurements that indicate progress against those objectives.

For example, a company has stated a strategic goal to improve market share relative to its competitors by offering a higher level of customer service. The company has determined that the ability to quickly resolve problems is a very important factor in determining customer loyalty and poor performance in this area has resulted in lost customers in the past, which has resulted in a degraded market share.

The company measures customer satisfaction annually and the measurement has shown a slight degradation in customer satisfaction, but it is not yet serious enough to cause any significant loss in revenue to its competitors. The assessment team decides that this metric is a lagging indicator of customer satisfaction because it is only measured annually and the way it is measured on a 7-point scale tends to make it somewhat insensitive to changes in customer satisfaction. The team decides to look for additional data that might be a more direct and timely indicator of how the company is doing in this area.

Process-level Metrics Example

Process-level metrics can provide a direct indication to the assessor of the effectiveness of a process being evaluated. Let's say the assessment team decides to drill down into process-level metrics in the customer service area.

The customer service organization tracks a metric called fix response time (FRT). The FRT metric measures the time it takes to resolve customer problems. The metric is expressed as a percentage of problems closed within an established window of time for minor and major problems as shown in Figure 10.8.

The data clearly show an indication of a problem in the middle of the chart; the percent of customer problems closed within the acceptable time

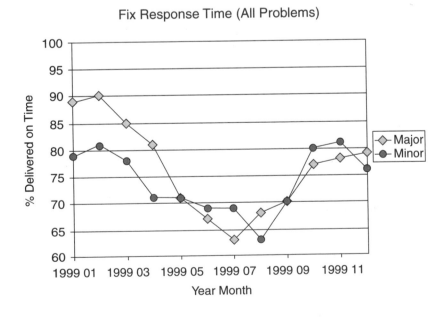

Figure 10.8   Process-level metric example.

limits for both major and minor problems has dropped to between 60 percent and 70 percent, which is probably unacceptable. Of course, one of the first questions to ask in this situation is what goal has been established for this metric and is this level of response acceptable to the customer? Let's assume for the sake of simplicity that an 80 percent closure rate is acceptable. If that is the case, there is clearly a problem.

This has now given the assessment team a clear indication of a potential problem that is an early indicator of customer satisfaction problems. (This data has been recently collected and has not impacted the annual customer satisfaction survey results.) By taking prompt and proactive corrective action now, the company might prevent this from becoming a much more serious problem that jeopardizes its most critical business goal of increasing market share relative to its competitors by improving customer satisfaction.

However, a metric like this is a good indicator of a problem, but it is like the oil temperature light on your car. If it goes off, you know you have a problem, but it doesn't give you enough information in itself to diagnose the problem. In this particular situation, there are a number of potential explanations of why this problem may have occurred:

- It is possible that the level of staffing during the summer months was insufficient to handle the load of customer problems due to vacations, and so on.

- It might be that the level of staffing was sufficient, but there may have been a significant increase in problems during that time for some reason (such as the introduction of a new product) that exceeded the ability of the staff to resolve issues in a timely manner.

- The problems that arose in that time might just have been more complex and took more time to resolve because of a design issue that needed to be corrected to fix the problem.

This particular metric creates what is called an *audit trail* in quality management terminology. An audit trail is a situation where an assessor sees there is a *potential* problem, but it requires more investigation to confirm that it is a problem and perhaps to further define the cause of the problem. In this example, for instance, the assessor would probably want to look further into the data by:

- Looking at samples of customer problems and staffing levels during the problem period to make a better determination of what was going on

- Evaluating any processes that are in place to ensure a satisfactory level of response to the customer and determining if the problem might be in the process itself or in the execution of the process

- Interviewing personnel to understand first-hand if the problem has been perceived by the staff and management of the department and if any corrective action has already been taken

This example illustrates how metrics can be used as an important tool by an assessment team to keep their evaluation focused on areas that really have significant impact on driving the company's business results.

Metrics have not been widely used in ISO 9000 style audits; the typical ISO 9000 audit is usually looking for compliance against requirements. In a continuous improvement environment, they take on added significance and are a very important tool that the assessor can use to keep the assessment focused on areas that add value to the business.

ENDNOTES

1. Malcolm Baldrige National Quality Award, *2003 Criteria for Performance Excellence* (2003).
2. Ibid.
3. Ibid.

11
Overall Summary

INTEGRATED SYSTEMS APPROACH

This book "paints the picture" of an evolving approach for integrating quality into the fabric of a business to drive business results. There has already been a considerable amount of evolution in the field of quality management over the years. As evidence of that, only a few years ago the American Society for Quality Control (ASQC) became the American Society for Quality (ASQ) to reflect a shift in emphasis from the traditional quality control approach to a broader emphasis on quality assurance.

However, the word *quality* itself continues to take on a broader meaning. It has historically been associated with reduction of defects. In today's world, we are moving beyond that definition. Producing defect-free products is only "table stakes" to play in the game; being competitive in today's world requires going well beyond that. In this world, "quality" includes:

- Reducing costs to make products that are not only free of defects, but also are highly competitive with similar products from other manufacturers

- Improving cycle time to get new products to market quickly to keep up with rapidly changing technologies

- Producing the right products that are well-aligned with customer needs and values

- Driving business results—quality is no longer something that can be delegated to the quality control department and companies should not pursue "quality for the sake of quality"

Many companies are beginning to call this *business excellence* rather than quality because it is such a major shift in emphasis and the term *quality* has such a well-established connotation that is typically associated with reduction of defects. The implications of implementing a well-integrated strategy for business excellence are very broad and you would probably see it differently depending on your role in the organization:

- A quality manager might see it from one perspective

- An information technology manager might see it from another perspective

- A human resources manager might see it from yet another perspective, and so on

It is like the old fable of the six blind men feeling the elephant:[1]

"It was six men of Indostan . . . To learning much inclined,
Who went to see the Elephant . . . Though all of them were blind,
That each by observation . . . Might satisfy his mind.

The First approached the Elephant . . . And, happening to fall
Against his broad and sturdy side . . . At once began to bawl:
"God bless me, but the Elephant . . . Is very like a wall!"

The Second, feeling the tusk . . . Cried, "Ho! what have we here
So very round and smooth and sharp? . . . To me 'tis very clear
This wonder of an Elephant . . . Is very like a spear!"

The Third approached the animal . . . And, happening to take
The squirming trunk within his hands . . . Thus boldly up he spake:
"I see," quoth he, "The Elephant . . . Is very like a snake!"

The Fourth reached out an eager hand . . . And felt about the knee:
"What most the wondrous beast is like . . . Is very plain," quoth he;
"Tis clear enough the Elephant . . . Is very like a tree!"

The Fifth, who chanced to touch the ear . . . Said, "Even the blindest man
Can tell what this resembles most . . . Deny the fact who can:
This marvel of an elephant . . . Is very like a fan!"

The Sixth no sooner had begun . . . About the beast to grope
Than, seizing on the swinging tail . . . That fell within his scope,

"I see," quoth he, "the Elephant . . . Is very like a rope!"

And so these men of Indostan . . . Disputed loud and long,
Each in his own opinion . . . Exceeding stiff and strong.
Though each was partly in the right . . . They all were in the wrong!

What is obviously needed is a cross-functional perspective that integrates these different views of how the business is designed and functions as a complete system. Most companies and the quality management community are not well prepared to implement this vision of the future for quality management.

Business and Organizational Issues

In many companies, there is a very large gap between the way the business is managed and the way quality is managed and the two are not well integrated. In many cases, functionally oriented organizations also make it difficult to achieve the cross-functional integration that is needed.

Overcoming these issues requires, at a minimum:

- Providing very strong overall leadership and direction to integrate the company around its mission, vision, and objectives

- Developing a cross-functional, "systems-thinking" perspective in all managers and appointing a cross-functional champion, if necessary, to facilitate and further integrate these functions

- Defining models, if necessary, to help all employees and managers understand the operation of the business from both an overall system and process perspective

- Creating a management approach, culture, and environment that is consistent with that approach and using broad-based communication and training throughout the company to achieve broad-based buy-in and support

Quality Management Issues

In the quality community, there are competing factions:

- There is the Baldrige faction, the ISO faction, the Six Sigma faction, and so on

- Each of these groups tends to see the problem through the lens of a particular approach to solving the problem

What is needed is to see the complementary nature of these different standards and process improvement approaches, and to understand how they all potentially contribute to achieving business excellence. Instead of attempting to redefine a business to fit a particular standard or approach, we need to focus on maximizing the effectiveness of the business and use whatever quality standards and process improvement approaches that may be appropriate as tools to achieve the business objectives.

New roles are probably needed to implement this vision. Within the quality management profession, there are two major roles:

1. The tactical role is associated with process control and ongoing quality control and quality assurance activities. This role is well understood and has been widely implemented.

2. The strategic role is associated with aligning all the tactical quality functions and process improvement initiatives with the company's business strategy, and providing high-level, cross-functional leadership to integrate these efforts not only within the enterprise, but also across an entire supply chain if necessary. This role is less well understood and not widely implemented.

It may not be called quality management, the individuals performing this role may do it informally, and they may have a background in a variety of different functional disciplines not limited to quality. What seems to be important in this role is applying sound systems thinking and an understanding of quality discipline, such as TQM, to achieve cross-functional integration. *This is the missing link in many companies that is required to develop a more integrated and cross-functional strategy.*

"The New CQO" by A. Blanton Godfrey correctly recognized how dramatically the role of the quality director is changing.[2] The job has expanded in three dimensions:

1. "First, the technical skills required continue to grow. Only a few years ago, the set of skills needed were defined as simple statistical methods, sampling and auditing, quality reporting, statistical process control, and understanding of testing and inspection. Knowing an industry's specific requirements was enough . . ."

2. "Second, the quality director must be an expert in quality culture, organizational dynamics, and change management. Often the most critical task for the director entails working with the senior management team to make radical changes in attitude and motivation, cross-functional working relationships, customer interactions, collaboration, and teamwork . . ."

3. "Third, the quality director must be an expert in business skills. Many quality directors now actively participate in strategic business planning and annual business operations planning."[3]

More Effectively Implementing Basic Quality Standards

In terms of the maturity levels discussed in chapter 9, it would be impossible for any company to advance beyond level 3 without some level of integration of their business management and quality management approach. Many companies may not be at that level of maturity but will still be able to use a systems approach to more effectively implement individual quality standards. The following are a few examples.

ISO 9000

In most cases, the reason ISO 9000 systems have not been more effective is not a problem with the standard itself; it is just poorly implemented.

- In many cases, companies do not take the time to understand how the standard applies to their business and how it can be used as a tool to improve effectiveness.

- In other cases, there is an insufficient level of senior management commitment and leadership to fully integrate the requirements of the standard into the way the business is managed, and it becomes an exercise to satisfy the auditors.

This situation would be typical of a company:

- That is at level 1 (see chapter 9 for definition of maturity levels) and has no quality standard or a very poorly implemented and/or ineffective quality standard

- That is at level 2 and has an effective ISO 9000:1994 implementation and wants to migrate to ISO 9000:2000 and create a focus on continuous improvement

Doing either of these transitions effectively requires some level of systems thinking but does not necessarily require full integration of the business and quality systems at this level of maturity.

Six Sigma

In other situations, quality standards and improvement methodologies like Six Sigma are implemented as a "program" and are overlaid on top of an existing organization without sufficiently understanding the operation of the business as a system or attempting to integrate the improvement methodology with the company's business strategy. For example,

- Companies adopt Six Sigma and simply define quotas for each organization to produce Six Sigma cost savings without fully integrating it into the way the business is managed. This would be characteristic of a company that is at a level 3 maturity level or below.

- Companies may attempt to use Six Sigma as a change program to redefine the company around Six Sigma rather than using these approaches as tools within the context of how their business system is defined to improve overall effectiveness.

What is needed is a focus on overall results, not just the activities needed to achieve those results. In many cases, the implementation of a quality system becomes the goal, when in fact it is only a tool for accomplishing a much larger goal. Relating individual activities within the organization to how they contribute to achieving overall results cannot be done effectively without an understanding of how the organization operates as a business system. These solutions have a limited chance for success as a quality program.

Synthesizing What We've Learned

There is a huge body of knowledge associated with effective business management that has been built up over the years; unfortunately, there has been a tendency to forget most of it and regard it as "obsolete" every time a new fad comes along. We need to break out of this approach and begin to synthesize many of the lessons that we have already learned:

- Peter Senge, for example, inspired a lot of my writing on the subject of systems thinking. Much of his work was done in the early 1990s and is still absolutely valid today, but people today seem to have forgotten about it and moved on to other things.

- TQM and reengineering are other examples of management "fads" that were very hot at one time but now have faded in popularity. In both cases, although there were some significant problems with the way they were implemented, most of the concepts behind both TQM and reengineering are still perfectly valid.

We need to learn from these earlier efforts and continue building the body of knowledge of how it all fits together instead of throwing everything away and starting over every time a new fad comes along.

The "Dotcom" era probably set back American management discipline by about five years and we are still recovering from it. Many companies "threw out the book" on what has been well-established, good business management practice and jumped on the technology of the Internet to fundamentally change the rules of the whole game:

- There was a tendency to think that all the rules of good business management had all of the sudden become obsolete. For example, you could put together a multimillion dollar business built on a foundation of a Web site and some marketing "hype" with little substance underneath it and an unclear plan of how it would ever become profitable.

- Good process management discipline went out of style. "We don't have time to define our processes because things are changing too rapidly and it will constrain our ability to grow fast enough to keep pace with the growth in the Internet."

That same "free-wheeling" management style has spilled over into some of the debacles we currently have with crises in financial accountability. We need to restore some basic good management discipline to American business.

These are all things that were common practice at one time that we have somehow forgotten about. We need to relearn some of these lessons before we can move forward.

BUSINESS SYSTEMS ENGINEERING

Fundamental Principles

All of the issues previously discussed point to the need for treating the business as a "system" and taking a systems engineering approach to design well-integrated business systems. Rapidly changing information technology will accelerate this trend and a new discipline is required to effectively implement this new technology. Like many other disciplines, there is no prescriptive approach on how to do business systems engineering; however, there are several important principles:

1. A Business Is a Complex System

    No single factor is more important for successfully applying business management concepts and quality standards than understanding that a business is a system. Many past failures can be attributed to:

- Underestimating the complexity of business systems and attempting to apply single dimension solutions to what is a multidimensional problem

- Applying a "fix" in one area without considering the potential for unintended impact in another area

- Failing to define and model a business system and to use that model as a baseline and framework for understanding its operation

2. Standards and Best Practices Should Help Design, Not Define, the System

One of the biggest mistakes companies make is to redefine their whole management system around a particular quality standard (for example, Baldrige or ISO). The role of these standards should not be to *define* the business management system; they are a "checklist" of items to consider in the design and should be used to validate the design. In the context of the systems engineering discipline discussed above, they are the "functional specs" that the design of the business management system should meet.

3. A Systems Approach Is Needed to Effectively Design Business Systems

If we were to design a complex system like the Space Shuttle, the approach would probably look something like the following:

- Start out with some kind of requirements and performance metrics of what it has to do (functional specifications for the Space Shuttle; business objectives and goals for the business)

- Decompose it into some sort of architectural building blocks people can understand (subsystem architecture for the Space Shuttle; enterprise model and core processes for the business)

- Further decompose the architectural building blocks into lower-level components (subsystem designs for the Space Shuttle; process maps for the business)

- Define some sort of test plan to validate that the system actually meets its performance requirements (flight test plan for the Space Shuttle; metrics for the business)

The steps for designing a management system would follow a similar approach:

1. Define the Enterprise Model

   Start with the strategy, mission, and purpose of the business and define the critical success factors the business must accomplish to be successful. Define the enterprise model and identify core processes.

2. Process Mapping

   Further break down each of the core processes into detailed process maps with assigned responsibilities and supporting resources.

3. Validate the Design of the System

   Finally, validate the design of the business system against any relevant standards and best practices to ensure that appropriate consideration has been given to all requirements. Then assess the performance of the processes in actual practice to determine their effectiveness in meeting applicable goals and requirements.

We are not well prepared to deal with this kind of systems engineering approach in the business environment and *the technology is advancing faster than our ability to effectively implement it.* What's needed is to accelerate the development of an approach and skills associated with an integrated approach to designing business processes and systems to keep pace with the changing technology of the information systems.

Methodology Overview

The general discipline and approach that is needed is essentially the same as the systems engineering discipline that has been used for designing complex systems for years; however, it has rarely been applied to business systems. That is probably because we think of business systems as being too simple to justify that kind of approach; but, in fact, that is probably not the case. If business systems are not already at that point, new information technology will certainly force that to happen very rapidly.

The benefits of a systems engineering approach are that it encourages a structured approach by focusing on the top-level system requirements and architecture as a first step before getting too far into the detailed design of any of the subsystems and components. To use a software analogy, if I set out to design some software and started by writing code without a clear idea of the overall architecture of the software, I would probably wind up with a tangled mess that's poorly organized and may or may not meet whatever requirements it was intended to meet.

A systems engineering approach treats the system as a whole as well as any subsystems that comprise the overall system initially as "black boxes." This approach allows focusing on the inputs and outputs of these "black boxes," and the factors that affect their performance at a high level without getting too far into the details of what goes on inside the "black boxes." Without that kind of approach, it is very easy to get lost in the details of the internal design of subsystems and components before the overall architecture and the interrelationships at a high level are defined and understood. Once the high-level design is understood, the design of the individual "black boxes" (subsystems) can be further decomposed to a lower level of detail.

Systems engineering has been widely used in the design of products for years. Extending this methodology to the design of business systems is relatively new. Table 11.1 shows a summary of how the two approaches generally compare. The systems engineering approach shown in this table for the design of products is only one possible approach for systems engineering and has been adapted from *Systems Engineering and Analysis* by Benjamin S. Blanchard and Walter F. Fabrycky.[4]

The following are some important notes to consider in using this model:

- The important thing to understand about this is the general concept of taking a complex system from a high-level view and progressively and gradually decomposing it into higher levels of detail as the design progresses.

- This is a conceptual model and in actual practice, the exact implementation of the methodology will likely vary considerably from one situation to the next.

- In reality, it is probably not a one-time, sequential approach as it is shown here. In a more typical scenario, it is probably more of an iterative process for arriving at an optimum design solution. (An iterative approach is typical in many cases in both a product development environment as well as a business systems environment.)

With an iterative process, the initial design of the business system would proceed to some point in the process, such as operational test and evaluation, and result in a first-pass design approach. Based on the information learned from that first-pass design, another pass through the design process might be initiated to further improve and refine the design.

Table 11.1 Comparison of systems engineering approach for products and business systems.

Design Stage	Product Design Approach		Business System Design Approach	
	Product Design Requirements	Design Output	Business System Design Requirements	Design Output
Conceptual design and advance planning phase	Needs Identification • Define the need that the product is intended to fill	• Market Requirements Document	Strategic Planning • Define the business strategy, including mission and vision • Identify target customers and their needs and values • Identify any external factors, such as technology and competition, that have a significant impact	• Strategic Plan
	• Requirements Analysis • Operational requirements • Maintenance and Support Concept • Evaluation of Feasible Technology Applications • Selection of Technical Approach	• System Specification	Business Planning • Define overall business goals and objectives • Identify key competitors and define competitive strategy • Define overall management approach, values, and principles for the business	• Business Plan
	• Functional Definition of System • Define system architecture, including major subsystems	• System Architecture	Enterprise Model Definition • Define core processes and interrelationships • Identify any best practices and standards that must be considered	• Enterprise Model

Continued

Note: The Program Plan/Project Plan is a living document that will be updated as the project progresses through each phase.

Table 11.1   *Continued*

Design Stage	Product Design Approach		Business System Design Approach	
	Product Design Requirements	**Design Output**	**Business System Design Requirements**	**Design Output**

	• System/Program Planning
	  • Define project plan for developing the product
	  • Identify team members that make up the design team
		• System Program/Project Plan*	• Business System Implementation Planning
			  • Define project plan for implementing the business system
			  • Define roles and responsibilities of the management team
				• Project Plan for Implementing Business System*

Preliminary design	• Functional Analysis
	• Requirements Allocation
	• Trade-off Studies
	• Synthesis
	• Preliminary Design
	• Test and Evaluation of Design Concepts (Early Prototyping)
		• Subsystem specifications	• Determine Core Process Requirements
			  • Goals and Metrics
			  • Interrelationships and interdependencies
			• Define overall Quality Management Strategy
			  • How will the overall system ensure high levels of quality and customer satisfaction?
				• Core Process Requirements

	• Acquisition Plans
	  • Contracting
	  • Program Implementation
	• Major Suppliers and Supplier Activities
		• Purchase Requirements	• Define Supply Chain Strategy and Supplier Requirements
			  • Who are the most critical suppliers?
			  • How will they be integrated into the design of the system?
				• Supply Chain Plan

Note: The Program Plan/Project Plan is a living document that will be updated as the project progresses through each phase.

Continued

Table 11.1

Design Stage	Product Design Approach		Business System Design Approach	
	Product Design Requirements	**Design Output**	**Business System Design Requirements**	**Design Output**
Detailed design and development	• Subsystem/Component Design • Trade-off studies and evaluation of alternatives • Development of engineering and prototype models • Verification of Manufacturing and Production Processes • Development Test and Evaluation • Supplier Activities • Production Planning	• Detailed Design Specifications	• Develop detailed process maps for all business processes • Determine and develop information systems requirements and define interrelationship to business processes • Determine and implement any external supplier requirements • Define the quality management plan, including the assessment approach and metrics, to evaluate the effectiveness of all business processes • Define all implementation and support requirements, including training • Define approach for ongoing process improvement	• Detailed process maps and system requirements • Plan for implementation and ongoing operation • Assessment approach and metrics • Process Improvement Methodology

Note: The Program Plan/Project Plan is a living document that will be updated as the project progresses through each phase.

Table 11.1

Design Stage	Product Design Approach		Business System Design Approach	
	Product Design Requirements	Design Output	Business System Design Requirements	Design Output
Production/ construction	• Production and/or Construction of System Components • Supplier Production Activities • Acceptance Testing • System Distribution and Operation • Developmental/Operational Test and Evaluation • Interim Contractor Support • System Assessment	• System Acceptance Testing	• Train all operational personnel and managers in the implementation of the process requirements • Deploy and test information systems requirements • Test and evaluate all business processes and systems in operational use • Evaluate effectiveness of business process design and take corrective action as necessary • Finalize design of all business processes and systems, and cutover to operational use	• Full Operational Implementation of Business Processes and Systems
Operational use and system support	• System Operation in the User Environment • Sustaining Maintenance and Logistic Support • Operational Testing • System Modifications for Improvement • Contractor Support • Systems Assessment (Field Data Collection and Analysis)	• Ongoing System Operation	• Track effectiveness of system performance against operational metrics and goals • Implement self-assessment process and process improvement methodology • Continue improving the system in operational use • Reengineer the system as required	• Successful Business System Operation Progress Against Goals • Successful Implementation of Process Improvement Methodology

Note: The Program Plan/Project Plan is a living document that will be updated as the project progresses through each phase.

From a business systems design perspective, the major steps in this process can be summarized as shown in Figure 11.1.

Figure 11.1   Overall business systems engineering process summary.

ENDNOTES

1. J. G. Saxe, *The Blind Men and the Elephant: John Godfrey Saxe's Version of the Famous Indian Legend* (New York: Whittlesley House, ca 1850).
2. A. B. Godfrey, "The New CQO," ASQ *Quality Progress* (April 1997): 17.
3. Ibid.
4. B. S. Blanchard and W. F. Fabrycky, *Systems Engineering and Analysis* (Upper Saddle River, NJ: Prentice Hall, 1998).

Appendix A
Lifecycle Model For Complex Improvement Initiatives

he following pages show a possible methodology for integrating the design and development of business processes and systems that can be used either by external consulting resources or by internal company resources. It is particularly appropriate for planning and managing complex business process improvement initiatives with a high level of systems and software development content.

The intent of this model is to show one possible approach for organizing a project for defining and implementing complex system solutions. In reading or using this model it's important to understand that this is only a model and not the *only* potential model for doing this. The important points to be considered are:

- The model can be entered at different points. The normal starting point is an understanding of the business requirements. If the company already feels confident that the business requirements are understood, the model can be entered at a later stage.

- The roles identified in this model are hypothetical. In the simplest case, many of them might be combined as needed (one person might perform several different roles).

- The complexity of the model needs to be adjusted so that it is appropriate to the risks, scope, and complexity of the overall effort.

BUSINESS STRATEGY AND REQUIREMENTS DEFINITION PHASE

Questions: How is the business doing? Where are the areas for improvement?

(This process assumes that the company's mission, strategy, and objectives have been defined as a starting point).

- Who are the key stakeholders (employees, customers, stockholders, partners, suppliers, and so on) that must be satisfied? What are their expectations? What are the most critical success factors for the business in meeting their expectations?
- What are the strengths and weaknesses of the company relative to other competitors? How can they gain strategic competitive advantage to increase customer satisfaction and market share?
- What are some of the best practices and standards in this industry/application area, and how would this company benefit from them?

Output

- Consensus on prioritized list of business and process areas for improvement
- Definition of critical success factors and metrics for measuring ongoing progress

Project Role	Tasks
Account Mgr/ Program Mgr	• Serve as a single point of contact at the business level • Use consultative approach to focus on the company's business and to lead the company through the solution process • Provide a single point of contact at a business level to manage communications and ensure successful completion of requirements • Lead the project team in developing initial proposal and gain commitment to the project
Project Mgr	• Plan and coordinate all resources required to meet project requirements • Develop initial action plan
Business Analyst	• Analyze business performance against metrics and perform gap assessment • Map business processes and audit processes, if necessary • Clearly identify weaknesses, areas for improvement, and disconnects • Define assessment model and goals for business process improvement • Identify and implement metrics required to monitor progress • Identify key issues that need to be overcome (for example, cultural issues, infrastructure issues, and so on) • Develop initial action plan for further effort • Build cross-functional consensus and commitment among company stakeholders

Project Role	Tasks
Systems Architect	• Provide input on potential technology solutions • Translate business requirements into architectural solution requirements

INFORMATION SYSTEMS ANALYSIS

Questions: What systems are in use? Are they effective?

- Are the systems well-aligned with the objectives of the business and with current and planned business processes?
- Are the systems effective in accomplishing their intended purpose?
- Are there opportunities to be gained by:
  - Higher levels of systems integration?
  - Replacing older systems with new technology to reduce costs and improve productivity?
  - Increased levels of process automation?
  - More effective sharing of documents and information across the enterprise?
  - Tighter coupling and sharing of information with selected partners and customers?
  - Better performance metrics and access to data?
- What are some of the constraints and issues that must be considered and overcome to successfully improve the current systems?
- Architectural issues, support issues, user familiarity, and training
- Resource, cost, and schedule constraints

Output

- Definition of current systems and architecture
- Recommended new system architecture
- Identification of major system requirements

Project Role	Tasks
Account Mgr/ Program Mgr	• Serve as a single point of contact at the business level
Project Mgr	• Serve as a single point of contact at the project level
Business Analyst	• Work with the systems architect to ensure that the architecture is consistent with business requirements
Systems Architect	• Analyze current systems and identify weaknesses as well as opportunities for improvement • Identify alternative solutions, evaluate tradeoffs, and identify the best solution approach

SOLUTION DEFINITION AND PROJECT PLANNING PHASE

Questions: Recommended solution? Cost to implement the solution? Resources required? Schedule? Risks?

- What architectures and products would provide a solution to improve the company's business systems?
- What tradeoffs must be considered in selecting the best approach? What is the best overall approach?
- What services will be needed to develop and implement the solution (application design, systems integration, training, implementation, ongoing support, and so on)?
- What are the major tasks that must be completed to design and implement the solution?
- What are some of the potential risks to be considered? How can they be mitigated?
- What are the critical dependencies that are essential to the success of the project?
- What are the resource and schedule requirements for completing each of the tasks? How can they be optimized?
- What are the roles and responsibilities of the various participants and stakeholders in the project? How will they be organized?
- What method will be used for communicating among the team, tracking progress and resolving any issues throughout the course of the project?
- How will the solution be tested and validated? What criteria are used for acceptance testing of the final solution?

Output

- Proposal describing solutions architecture and implementation requirements
- Project plan with cost, schedule, resource estimates, risks, and dependencies for design and implementation of the solution

Project Role	Tasks
Account Mgr/ Program Mgr	• Serve as a single point of contact at the business level
Project Mgr	• Serve as a single point of contact at the project level • Identify and plan all tasks that need to be performed • Identify resource and schedule requirements • Identify risks and plan mitigation strategies, as necessary • Document overall project plan as well as requirements
Business Analyst	• Work with the project team to ensure that the project proposal and plan is consistent with business requirements
Systems Architect	• Provide input to the project plan on design and implementation requirements
Design Engineer	• Provide input on any special design requirements
Implementation	• Provide input on implementation requirements • Develop implementation plan, if necessary

Project Role	Tasks
Training	• Provide input on training requirements • Develop training plan if necessary
Ongoing Support	• Provide input on ongoing support requirements • Develop ongoing support plan, if necessary

SOLUTION DESIGN PHASE

Questions: What is the best approach to designing the solution requirements?

- What technologies are available to design and implement the solution? Pros and cons of each?
- Final design approach?
- How can the solution be optimized to best meet operational requirements and minimize implementation requirements?

Output

- Completed system design

Project Role	Tasks
Account Mgr/ Program Mgr	• Serve as a single point of contact at the business level • Manage any changes in scope with the company
Project Mgr	• Serve as a single point of contact at the project level • Manage the project execution, conduct project reviews, and provide status reporting to the company as required • Track and resolve any project issues to ensure successful completion of the project
Business Analyst	• Participate in design reviews and testing as necessary to ensure design is consistent with company business requirements
Systems Architect	• Participate in design reviews as necessary to ensure design is consistent with architectural requirements
Design Engineer	• Analyze design alternatives • Develop applicable specifications • Testing strategy and test plan • Complete all design tasks • Document and test the solution
Implementation	• Ensure that any design impact on implementation requirements is well understood and planned
Training	• Ensure that any design impact on training requirements is well understood and planned
Ongoing Support	• Ensure that any design impact on ongoing support requirements is well understood and planned

SOLUTION IMPLEMENTATION AND VALIDATION PHASE

Questions

- What are the implementation requirements?
- What are the installation and configuration requirements?
- What are the user training requirements?
- What are the testing and operational cutover requirements?
- What resources are required to complete the implementation requirements?

Output

- System cutover and acceptance for operational use

Project Role	Tasks
Account Mgr/ Program Mgr	• Serve as a single point of contact to the company at the business level
Project Mgr	• Serve as a single point of contact to the company at the project level • Manage the solution acceptance process with the company • Coordinate all resources required to fulfill implementation requirements
Business Analyst	• Provide support as required to ensure solution is consistent with requirements
Systems Architect	• Provide support as required to ensure solution is consistent with requirements
Design Engineer	• Conduct final acceptance testing of the system
Implementation	• Perform implementation requirements
Training	• Perform training requirements
Ongoing Support	• Participate in cutover and acceptance testing to ensure a smooth transition to ongoing support

Appendix B
Additional Recommended Reading, Resources, and Tools

The following is a partial list of recommended reading, resources, and tools to support the materials in this book. Please refer to the Web site address http://www.bizexgroup.comfor a more up-to-date and complete list.

The Business Excellence Group sponsors this site, which contains links to additional reading, resources, services, and tools to help implement the capabilities in this book.

Membership in the Business Excellence Group is open to companies that provide tools and services in support of achieving business excellence, as well as any company that wishes to share knowledge and experience in this area with others. The members of the Business Excellence Group subscribe to the common notion that achieving high levels of excellence in business requires taking an integrated view of functions and processes that comprise the business.

ADDITIONAL RECOMMENDED READING

Balanced Scorecard
Robert S. Kaplan and David P. Norton. *The Balanced Scorecard.* Cambridge, MA: Harvard Business School Press, 1996.

Business Excellence
Jim Collins. *Good To Great.* New York: HarperCollins Publishers, 2001.

Business Process Reengineering

Michael Hammer and James Champy. *Reengineering the Corporation: A Manifesto for Business Revolution.* New York: Harper Business, 2001.

Michael Hammer. *Beyond Reengineering.* New York: HarperCollins Publishers, 1996.

Customer Value

Barry Sheehy, Hyler Bracey, and Rick Frazier. *Winning the Race for Value.* New York: American Management Association, 1996.

Bradley T. Gale. *Managing Customer Value.* New York: Free Press, 1994.

Michael Treacy and Fred Wiersena. *Discipline of Market Leaders.* Reading, MA: Addison-Wesley, 1995.

Information Technology—ERP Systems

Charles G. Cobb. "Enterprise Resource Planning (ERP) Systems," March 1998. For downloadable copy, go to http://www.bizexgroup.com.

Information Technology—Standards-Based Systems

Charles G. Cobb, David A. Kopcso, and William Rybolt. "Building Standards-Based Business Processes and Systems." CIMS Working Paper Series #2002-04, March 2002. For downloadable copy, go to http://www.bizexgroup.com.

ISO 9000

ANSI/ISO/ASQ Q9004-2000 Quality management systems—Guidelines for performance improvement. Milwaukee: ASQ Quality Press. 2000.

ANSI ISO/ASQ Q9000-2000 *Quality managment systems— fundamentals and vocabulary.* Milwaukee: ASQ Quality Press. 2000.

ANSI ISO/ASQ Q9001-2000 *Quality managment systems— Requirements.* Milwaukee: ASQ Quality Press. 2000.

Knowledge Management

Carla O'Dell and C. Jackson Grayson Jr. *If Only We Knew What We Know.* New York: Free Press, 1998.

Charles G. Cobb. "Knowledge Management and Quality Systems." Paper presented to the AQC 2000 Conference in Indianapolis, IN

May 2000. For downloadable copy go to
http://www.bizexgroup.com.

Davenport, Thomas et al. "How Can Organizations Use Knowledge
More Effectively?" *Sloan Management Review* (winter 1998).

David A. Garvin. "Building a Learning Organization." *Harvard Business Review on Knowledge Management,* 1998, p. 52.

Leadership

James M. Kouzes and Barry Z. Posner. *The Leadership Challenge.*
San Francisco: Jossey-Bass, 1995.

Metrics

Robert S. Kaplan and David P. Norton. *The Balanced Scorecard.*
Cambridge, MA: Harvard Business School Press, 1996.

Process Management

Thomas H. Davenport. *Process Innovation.* Cambridge, MA: Harvard
Business School Press, 1993.

Strategic Planning

Jim Collins. *Good To Great.* New York: HarperCollins, 2001.

Robert S. Kaplan and David P. Norton. *The Balanced Scorecard.*
Cambridge, MA: Harvard Business School Press, 1996.

Systems Engineering

Benjamin S. Blanchard and Walter F. Fabrycky. *Systems Engineering
and Analysis.* Upper Saddle River, NJ: Prentice Hall, 1998.

Norman B. Reilly. *Team Based Product Development Guidebook.*
Milwaukee: ASQ Quality Press, 1999.

Total Quality Management (TQM)

Stephen George and Arnold Weimershirch. *Total Quality Management.* New York: John Wiley & Sons, 1994.

ADDITIONAL RESOURCES AND TOOLS

Designing management systems for business excellence can be difficult
without the appropriate resources and tools. Examples include:

- Assessment tools designed for continuous improvement

- Process mapping and enterprise modeling tools

A list of additional resources and tools is available at the Web site http://www.breakthroughsolns.com/BE/Index.htm to supplement the material in this text.

Appendix C
Acronyms and Glossary of Terms

Baldrige—Malcolm Baldrige National Quality Award (MBNQA)

A U.S. quality award and assessment criteria used to evaluate business excellence that is administered by the National Institute of Standards and Technology (NIST) (see chapter 2 for additional information).

Business Excellence—Business excellence is a new and emerging view of quality in the context of a business organization.

Businesses that have successfully implemented a business excellence strategy have made quality an integral part of the way the business is designed. It goes beyond the quality of products and services and takes on a broader meaning of maximizing the effectiveness of the business in meeting or exceeding customer value expectations and using continuous improvement to drive business results. It is the total quality of how the business operates as a system.

Business Process Reengineering (BPR)—The *fundamental* rethinking and *radical* redesign of the business *processes* to achieve *dramatic* improvements in critical, contemporary measures of performance.[1]

Business Systems Engineering—The application of systems engineering principles to create an integrated methodology for designing business processes that considers all aspects of the business as a system.

ERP—Enterprise resource planning systems

"A business management system that integrates all facets of the business, including planning, manufacturing, sales, and marketing."[2] The goal of an ERP system is to tightly integrate the definition of the business processes and information systems and provide a common language and frame of reference for seamless exchange of information across the enterprise. Most ERP systems include standard "blueprints" for common business processes (see chapter 2 for additional information).

ISO 9000—A widely recognized family of international standards used in quality management since 1987. The ISO 9000 family of standards includes the individual standards shown in Table C.1.

The ISO 9000 family of standards has several industry-specific derivatives:

- QS-9000 is an example that has been widely adopted throughout the automotive industry (it is now being converted to TS-16949).

- AS-9000 has been adopted in the aerospace industry.

- TL 9000 has been developed for the telecommunications industry.

- Consideration is being given to create a new standard based on ISO 9000 for the financial services industry.

The ISO 9000 family of standards was originally developed primarily from a process control perspective (see chapter 2 for additional information).

Table C.1   ISO 9000 standards family.

Standard	Title
ISO 9000	*Quality management systems—Fundamentals and vocabulary*
ISO 9001:1994	*Quality systems—Model for quality assurance in design, development, production, installation and servicing* (Replaced by ISO 9001:2000)
ISO 9002:1994	*Quality systems—Model for quality assurance in production, installation and servicing* (Replaced by ISO 9001:2000)
ISO 9003:1994	*Quality systems—Model for quality assurance in final inspection and test* (Replaced by ISO 9001:2000)
ISO 9001:2000	*Quality management systems—Requirements*
ISO 9004:2000	Quality management systems—Guidelines for performance improvements

Note: All standards available through ASQ Quality Press.

Knowledge Management (KM)—

"Knowledge management is the strategy and processes to enable the creation and flow of relevant knowledge throughout the business to create organizational, customer, and consumer value." David Smith, Unilever[3]

"Knowledge management is the broad process of locating, organizing, transferring, and using the information and expertise within an organization. The overall knowledge management process is supported by four key enablers: leadership, culture, technology, and measurement." American Productivity and Quality Center[4]

Six Sigma—An improvement methodology that was originally developed by Motorola (see chapter 6 for additional information).

TQM—Total Quality Management

"TQM is a business philosophy related to an organization's management system that:

- Seeks to improve the results, including the financial performance

- Guarantees long-term survival through a consistent focus on improving customer satisfaction

- Meets the needs of all its stakeholders (customers, employees, owners, and suppliers)

Overall, TQM:

- Institutionalizes a never-ending process of improvement

- Emphasizes and is driven by the need to meet and exceed customer needs and expectations

- Works to eliminate waste and rework

- Harnesses the brainpower of all people in the organization

Further, TQM focuses on:

- External factors, including the customer, competition, and society

- Management leadership and commitment

- Employee participation and empowerment

- Sensitivity to the needs of internal and external customers

- Continuous improvement of processes, products, and services

- Fact-based decision making

The critical aspects of TQM are its customer orientation, its emphasis on continuous improvement, and its organizationwide aspects—the participation of all members of the organization aiming, together, at long-term success through customer satisfaction.

Process management embraces a systems approach to management and a holistic view of the organization. An organization is seen as a unified, purposeful system composed of interrelated processes. Instead of dealing with functional activities, process management advocates managing the system by process hierarchy—across boundaries as the work gets done."[5]

XML—Extensible Markup Language

In simple terms, XML is to data what HTML (Hypertext Markup Language) is to text. XML provides a standardized way to describe the structure and content of data of any level of complexity from a single data item or record to a complete database.

XML can be used by businesses to standardize the format of documents and data, such as purchase orders, requests for quotation, or any other kind of business information. In XML, the structure and content of the data are independent of the format by which the data are displayed or presented. For example, two different companies might have purchase order formats that look completely different, but that have exactly the same data structure. These two companies do have to agree on the schema of the data that is to be exchanged; however, one of the characteristics of an XML document is that the document defines the schema of the data as well as the values of the data.

ENDNOTES

1. M. Hammer and J. Champy, *Reengineering the Corporation: A Manifesto for Business Revolution* (1993).
2. "ERP Definition," http://www.pcwebopedia.com/ERP.htm.
3. "Quotes on Knowledge Management," Web site: http://wbln0018.worldbank.org/HRS/yournet.nsf/yournet/DynaFrame? OpenDocument&Page=7FC464245C5B04208525687E00522999.
4. Ibid.
5. ASQC Body of Knowledge, 1997.

Index